the Easy Family Cookbook

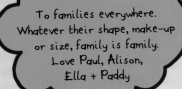

To families everywhere.
Whatever their shape, make-up
or size, family is family.
Love Paul, Alison,
Ella + Paddy

First published in Great Britain
in 2017 by Hamlyn, a division of
Octopus Publishing Group Ltd,
Carmelite House,
50 Victoria Embankment,
London EC4Y 0DZ

www.octopusbooks.co.uk

An Hachette UK Company
www.hachette.co.uk

ISBN 9780600631859

A CIP catalogue record for this book is available
from the British Library

Typeset in Cooper Light and Ella's Kitchen®

Printed and bound in China

Created by Ella's Kitchen and Harris + Wilson

10 9 8 7 6 5 4 3 2 1

Recipe developer: Nicola Graimes
Photographer: Jonathan Cherry
Art direction, design + styling: Anita Mangan
Managing editor: Judy Barratt
Project manager for Ella's Kitchen: Angie Turner
Photoshoot direction: Sarah Ford + Manisha Patel
Recipe editor: Wendy Hobson
Assistant production manager: Lucy Carter
Design assistant: Ewa Lefmann
Illustrator: Shareef Ali
Jacket illustration: Havas Worldwide London
Home economists: Rosie Reynolds, Jayne Cross
+ Kitty Coles

Disclaimer

A few recipes include nuts, seeds and nut
derivatives. Nuts and seeds pose a choking risk for
young children – always chop or blend nuts and
seeds before serving, as appropriate to your child's
age. Anyone with a known nut allergy, or with a
family history of allergy, should consult their doctor
before giving nuts to their baby for the first time.

Honey should not be given to children under
the age of 12 months.

Take every care when cooking with and for
children. Neither the author, the contributors
nor the publisher can accept any liability for any
consequences arising from the use of this book,
or the information contained herein.

Publisher's notes

Standard level spoon measures are used:

1 tablespoon = one 15 ml spoon
1 teaspoon = one 5 ml spoon

Both metric and imperial measurements are given.
Use one set of measurements, not a mixture of both.

Ovens should be preheated to the specified
temperature. For fan-assisted ovens, follow the
manufacturer's instructions to adjust cooking times
and temperatures.

Medium-sized ingredients and pans and medium-
strength cheese are used throughout unless
specified. Herbs are fresh unless specified.

Use low-salt stock, and avoid adding salt to recipes.

the Easy Family Cookbook

100 yummy + easy recipes
that big + little eaters will love

hamlyn

Contents

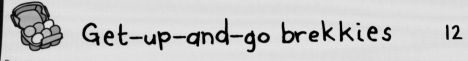

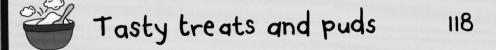
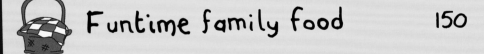

Foreword by Ella's dad

When I think about family mealtimes, I see my young self with my parents and my brother around the same table; I see my own kids and my wife and the myriad occasions that we have sat together to eat. I think of those special occasions when, often with others, we have celebrated a birthday or an achievement.

Alison and I have always put the highest value on organizing our lives so that we can have as many family meals with Ella and Paddy as possible. Ella talks about the security of our Sunday pancakes routine, and Paddy enjoys getting involved in the day-to-day cooking. They have memories that hinge on family mealtime experiences – like the time we made a warming stew to eat outside in the February snow! And the time a trained cook came to Ella's birthday party and used garlic butter in the cookies. YUCK!

Ella and Paddy have become talented cooks, which I am sure is partly down to our family culture of offering them what we want to eat and of eating together. It hasn't always worked: I can think of meals they've walked away from having barely eaten a thing – but they survived! It's much easier to cook one meal for everyone and it's worth being brave. With that in mind, we hope this book will optimize both your own time and your quality family time. Alison, Ella, Paddy and I, along with the whole Ella's Kitchen gang, hope you enjoy using the recipes as much as we enjoyed creating them.

Keep smiling,

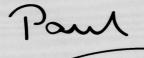

Paul, Ella's dad
Follow me on Twitter: @Paul_Lindley

Our easy family cookbook

A bit about using this book

At Ella's Kitchen we love it when families enjoy good food – from choosing what to cook and shopping for the ingredients to making the meal and spending time around the table – together. These shared experiences teach little ones that mealtimes are about more than just what they're eating. They learn that food creates social occasions during which we can share stories, connect with each other, and have fun! We believe that if children learn from a young age that good food is for everyone and that mealtimes are positive experiences, they'll go on to develop a healthy love of food that will last a lifetime.

Look out for our handy pull-out meal planner and 'What shall we eat today?' guide – use them to help plan your week around the family table.

Feeding a family

We know, though, that it's not always practical for everyone to sit around the table to eat at the same time every day. As well as recipes that are good to eat together, we've included lots that we hope are brilliant for when you need to feed the kids an early tea, and keep portions back for the grown-ups to eat later. Every recipe tells you how many it's intended to feed (see icons, page 9). Serves 4, for example, approximates for two adults, one hungry older child and one toddler. However, every family and every appetite is different. You know your family best, so use your judgement and adjust the quantities to suit.

We researched it!

We commissioned the British Nutrition Foundation to review lots of studies about the best ways to help children develop a healthy relationship with food. The Foundation found that involving children in cooking, and eating together as a family can help to establish healthy eating habits. Encouraging children to explore and play with food using all their senses was also found to help.

Babies can join in, too!

Once weaning is established (that is, you've moved on from offering your baby simple veg or fruit purées), look for the recipes with the special bowl icons (see box, opposite), as these are recipes you can blend or mash just as they are (we've listed the 10 month recipes in our pull-out, too) to give to the littlest members of your family. Occasional pop-up boxes give you pointers on how to adapt other recipes for babies. Use your judgement when deciding what is suitable to feed your baby, and remember:

☺ Mash, blend or chop all food to the texture suitable for your baby's age and stage – adding a little cooking water or their usual milk, if necessary.

☺ Before your baby reaches six months old, avoid all dairy or other allergens, such as gluten, egg, soya and nuts.

☺ Until your baby is 12 months old, cook unpasteurized cheeses, including parmesan, and don't give him or her runny eggs or any honey.

☺ For older babies, even past 12 months, leave out nuts and seeds if you think they might pose a choking risk, or chop or grind them very finely until you're confident they're just right.

The best ingredients

All of our recipes have been approved by the Ella's Kitchen nutritionist. We've avoided adding extra salt or refined sugar, and instead we've used lots of herbs, spices and natural sweeteners (such as honey and maple syrup), to make sure everything is *reeeally* tasty, but also as good for you as it can possibly be. When we can't avoid using sugar (like in some of the treat recipes), we've always reduced the overall sugar content so that even the treats and cakes are better for you. Yippee!

We recommend that you use organic foods, especially for fresh ingredients. We believe that organic farmers produce their foods using the purest farming standards and that organic farming is better for the planet.

Finally, all the ingredients should be available in your local supermarket and you may even have lots of them in your cupboards already.

Key to icons

At the top of every recipe, you'll find a combination of the following symbols to help make feeding your family as easy as it can be.

makes
How many pieces the recipe makes

serves
How many family members the recipe serves

prep
How long the ingredients take to prepare

cook
How long the recipe takes to cook

freeze me
Whether the recipe (or part of it) is suitable for freezing

Baby age bowls:
Suitable from 7 months old
Suitable from 10 months old

Fun family mealtimes

We all know that little ones pick up even the teeniest habits from us as they watch and learn. Eating together is a great way to embed some good eating practices – from the importance of munching on veggies and exploring food with all our senses to how to hold cutlery and to chew before swallowing! Here are our top tips for making sure family mealtimes are as fun and as positive as can be.

Research from Harvard University in the USA shows that the best way to boost a child's vocabulary is to talk to them at teatime. Take a look at our activity on pages 102–103 for some ideas to get the conversation flowing.

Get everyone involved!

Learning to love food is not just about eating: getting little ones involved in buying, preparing and cooking it from an early age is important, too. Find your local pick-your-owns, visit local farmers' markets (marvel at the colours and smells, perhaps even have a few tasters), and use a trip to your supermarket as a voyage of discovery. The more you do together, the more your whole family will feel part of the foody gang, and so all-the-more excited about what you eat.

Cooking together is especially important. Even toddlers can help roll, weigh and stir, and lots more! Look out for our *Can I Help?* boxes throughout the book for other ideas on how to make cooking together part of your family time.

Keep feet on the ground!

Research suggests that if a little person's feet dangle, he or she will feel imbalanced and is more likely to fidget. If your little one's feet don't touch the floor at the table, pop a box underneath them as a foot rest, or come down to 'little' level and eat around the coffee or play table.

Inspire good little eaters

Lots of our Ella's Friends ask us how to help little ones learn to love a wider range of food. Here are our top tips:

☺ **Do nothing** When mealtimes become a battleground, they stop being fun. Tell any fussy eaters that it's fine to leave their meal, but they must still sit at the table with you while you eat yours. Hold your nerve – most little ones will start to nibble on something (and then gradually more and more) if only to pass the time…

☺ **Give little ones some control** If you're preparing a veg that can come several ways, allow them to choose which way (potatoes can be boiled, mashed or baked; carrots can be raw or cooked, and so on). Present veggies on a dish to allow self-service – offer three kinds with a deal that everyone must choose at least two to eat. (You can use leftovers in stews and sauces.)

☺ **Keep portion sizes small and appropriate** Little people have little tummies – an overloaded plate can feel off-putting. Offer small amounts with the option for more (and lots of praise) when it's all gone.

Make time!

Mealtimes may not always be able to include every member of your family, but try thinking of some creative ways to have more meals together than you do now. For example, if one of you works, could you all meet for lunch (a picnic is lovely) near the workplace? Could you have breakfast together – even if it means getting up 15 minutes earlier? If you can't have weekday family teatimes, are there evenings when just one of you could eat with the little ones? And, of course, earmark a time (probably at the weekend) when you all promise to eat a whole meal together. It might be Saturday supper or Sunday lunch, but whenever it is schedule that time as an appointment that you always do your best to keep.

No distractions!

Mealtimes are the perfect times to be together. Turn off the television, put away all smartphones and tablets, and make sure all little people have been to the toilet before you start. Talk about the food, engaging all the senses (what does it look like? How does it smell? How does it feel? What does it taste like?), talk about the day. Try to make sure everyone gets a turn to talk, respond and share.

Crunchy coconut + cranberry granola

makes
16
servings

prep
10
minutes

cook
30
minutes

Homemade baked granola makes a crunchy, munchy and moreish start to the day for everyone. And it's not just for breakfast – check out all the other yummy ways to eat it in the box below.

What you need

250 g/9 oz **jumbo rolled porridge oats**

100 g/3½ oz **pecan nuts**

55 g/2 oz **hazelnuts**

100 g/3½ oz **mixed seeds**, such as pumpkin, sunflower, sesame and linseeds

1 tablespoon **ground cinnamon**

5 generous tablespoons **coconut oil**

100 ml/3½ fl oz **maple syrup** or **clear honey**

1 teaspoon **vanilla extract**

40 g/1½ oz unsweetened **desiccated coconut**

100 g/3½ oz **dried cranberries**, chopped if large

Yogurt or **whole milk** and **fresh fruit**, to serve

What to do

1. Preheat the oven to 170°C/325°F/Gas Mark 3. Mix together the oats, nuts, seeds and cinnamon in a large bowl.

2. Melt the coconut oil in a saucepan over a low heat, then stir in the maple syrup or honey and the vanilla. Pour it into the bowl with the oat mixture and stir well until everything is combined.

3. Tip the granola mixture onto two baking trays, spreading it out in an even layer, then bake for 20 minutes. Remove the trays from the oven and stir in the desiccated coconut. Return the trays to the oven and cook for another 10 minutes until everything is light golden and crisp. Remove from the oven and stir in the cranberries, then leave to cool and crisp up a bit more. Chop any large nuts, as necessary; and for young children, blitz in a food processor or chop finely before serving. Serve the granola with yogurt or milk and topped with fresh fruit. Store any remaining granola in an airtight jar for up to 10 days.

Anytime, anyhow!

This granola is great for nibbling on just as it is, as a snack. Or, try slicing a banana, rolling the slices in the granola and freezing them for something chilly. You can stir it into yogurt or sprinkle it over a salad or pancakes, knead it into bread dough before baking, or add it to a smoothie before whizzing!

Palm tree porridge

serves **4** · prep **10** minutes · cook **10** minutes

Our quick-and-easy porridge has a dash of sunshine in the form of coconut milk and tasty tropical mango.

What you need

150 g/5½ oz **porridge oats**

600 ml/1 pint **coconut drinking milk**, plus extra to serve

½ teaspoon **ground cinnamon**, plus extra for sprinkling

1 **small mango**, peeled, stoned and cut into cubes

1 tablespoon **mixed seeds**, toasted

1 tablespoon **coconut flakes**, toasted

What to do

1. Put the oats, coconut drinking milk and 575 ml/18 fl oz water in a saucepan, stir, and bring to the boil over a medium heat. Stir in the cinnamon, then reduce the heat to low, part-cover with a lid and simmer for 8–10 minutes, stirring, until creamy.

2. If you are serving to young children, finely chop the mango, toasted seeds and coconut flakes.

3. Spoon the porridge into bowls and sprinkle with the extra cinnamon, the chopped mango, and the toasted seeds and coconut. Pour extra milk over the porridge, to serve.

Love your leftovers!

Turn any leftover porridge into a tasty snack: leave it to cool, then cut it into fingers and pan-fry in butter until golden and crisp on the outside. Lovely!

From 10 months

For babies

Leave out the seeds and mash up the mango. Remember to check the temperature before serving!

Spiced brekkie hash-up

 serves 4
 prep 10 minutes
 cook 20 minutes
 freeze me
 10+ (hash only)

A hash is a brilliant way to use up leftover potatoes and veggies. We love it for breakfast topped with an egg, and with a sprinkling of curry powder to make it tingle on the tongue!

What you need

3 tablespoons **sunflower oil**, plus extra for cooking eggs

500 g/1 lb 2 oz **cooked potatoes**, cubed

1 **onion**, sliced

250 g/9 oz **cooked sprouts**, halved or quartered, or **white cabbage**, finely shredded

2 **garlic** cloves, chopped

140 g/5 oz **halloumi cheese**, cubed

1 heaped teaspoon **mild curry powder**

1 teaspoon **cumin seeds** (optional)

4 **eggs** (optional)

What to do

1. Heat the oil in a large frying pan over a medium heat. Add the potatoes and onion and cook for 10 minutes, stirring often, until the onion has softened and the potatoes are light golden.

2. Add the sprouts or cabbage, garlic, halloumi, curry powder and cumin, if using, stir until combined, then cook for another 5 minutes, turning regularly, until everything is heated through.

3. If serving topped with a fried egg, put the hash in the oven (set to a low temperature) to keep warm, covering it with a plate to stop it drying out. Heat enough oil to cover the base of the frying pan and fry the eggs as you like them, then serve on top of the hash.

 Just for fun

Around the world!

Herbs and spices are brilliant for a foody adventure. Gather together four spices and herbs with a distinctive smell – cumin, lemongrass, basil and cinnamon make a good start. What countries do they make you think of? (For these, we think India, Thailand, Italy and Morocco.) Show your little one where these places are on a map – food isn't from the supermarket, but all over the world!

Awesome apple hotcakes

makes 10 · prep 10 minutes + resting · cook 20 minutes · freeze me

These fluffy little American-style pancakes have apple goodness all the way through, and a pinch of cinnamon for added zing. Topped with berries and lashings of creamy yogurt, they are a special morning treat.

What you need

115 g/4 oz **self-raising flour**

1 teaspoon **baking powder**

1 **egg**, beaten

175 ml/6 fl oz **buttermilk**

3–4 tablespoons **whole milk**

1 tablespoon **maple syrup** or **clear honey**, plus extra for drizzling

1 teaspoon **vanilla extract**

1 **eating apple** (skin on), cored and coarsely grated

½ teaspoon **ground cinnamon**

Unsalted butter or **sunflower oil**, for cooking

Fruit and **natural yogurt**, to serve

What to do

1. Sift the flour and baking powder into a large bowl and mix together.

2. Whisk together the egg, buttermilk, milk, maple syrup or honey and vanilla in a jug, then gradually whisk it into the flour mixture to make a fairly thick batter. Leave to rest for 20 minutes (or overnight, if easier).

3. Stir the grated apple and cinnamon into the batter, adding a splash more milk if the batter seems too thick. It should be about the thickness of double cream.

4. Heat enough butter or oil to lightly grease the base of a large frying pan over a medium heat. Add 3 or 4 individual ladlefuls of batter (about 3 tablespoons per hotcake) into the pan to cook 3 or 4 hotcakes at a time. Cook the hotcakes for 4–6 minutes, turning once, until golden and set. Keep warm in a low oven while you make 10 hotcakes in total.

5. Serve the hotcakes topped with fruit and yogurt, then drizzled with a little extra maple syrup or honey.

Buttermilk know-how

You can usually find buttermilk in cartons in most supermarket chillers. If you can't find it, you can substitute with the same quantity of yogurt mixed with 1 teaspoon of lemon juice.

Champion's buckwheat pancakes

serves 4–6 | prep 10 minutes + resting | cook 20 minutes | freeze me (cooked pancakes)

All champions need energy, and buckwheat, which is gluten free, contains lots of fibre and magnesium, which our bodies need to make energy. Served with spinach, too, this is a breakfast with plenty of get-up-and-go!

What you need

115 g/4 oz **buckwheat flour**

1 **egg**, lightly beaten

300 ml/½ pint **whole milk**

30 g/1 oz **unsalted butter**, melted

Sunflower oil, for cooking

For the filling

20 g/¾ oz **unsalted butter**

350 g/12 oz **baby spinach leaves**, tough stalks removed

4 tablespoons **cream cheese**

A good squeeze of **lemon** juice

What to do

1. To make the pancake batter, sift the flour into a large bowl and make a well in the centre. In a separate bowl, mix together the egg, milk and butter, then gradually whisk the wet mixture into the flour to make a smooth batter. Leave to rest for 1 hour.

2. While the batter is resting, make the filling. Melt the butter in a saucepan, add the spinach and cook for a few minutes, turning, until wilted. Stir in the cream cheese and a good squeeze of lemon juice, to taste. Turn until everything is combined and warmed through, adding a splash of water, if needed. Cover with a lid and set aside.

3. To cook the pancakes, heat a large, dry frying pan over a medium heat, then add a splash of sunflower oil and carefully wipe off any excess with a crumpled sheet of kitchen paper. Add a ladleful of batter and swirl the pan until the batter coats the base. Cook for 2–3 minutes, turning once, until set and golden. Keep warm in a low oven while you fry the remaining pancakes, making about 4–6 large pancakes in total.

4. Gently reheat the filling, if needed, and spoon it on top of the pancakes. Serve flat or folded in half.

23

Zoomy mushrooms

serves 4 | prep 5 minutes | cook 10 minutes | 10+

These creamy mushrooms make a speedy cooked breakfast. Served on toasted rye bread they will keep rumbly tummies nicely filled up until lunchtime.

What you need

1 tablespoon **olive oil**

15 g/½ oz **unsalted butter**

350 g/12 oz **chestnut mushrooms**, sliced, or **small button mushrooms**

1 **garlic** clove, chopped

1 teaspoon **thyme** leaves, plus extra for sprinkling

6 tablespoons **whole milk**, plus extra if needed

2 tablespoons **crème fraîche**

½ teaspoon **Dijon mustard**

1–2 teaspoons **lemon** juice, to taste

4 slices of **rye bread**, toasted

Freshly ground **black pepper**

1 tablespoon snipped **chives**, to serve

What to do

1. Heat the oil and butter in a large frying pan over a medium heat. When the butter has melted, add the mushrooms and cook for 5 minutes, turning them continuously, or until any liquid released by the mushrooms has evaporated.

2. Reduce the heat to medium–low, add the garlic and thyme and cook for 1 minute, stirring. Add the milk, crème fraîche, mustard and lemon juice, then cook for another 1 minute or so, stirring, until everything is warmed through. Add a little extra milk, if needed, and season with a little pepper.

3. Spoon the mushrooms on top of the toasted rye bread and serve sprinkled with chives and extra thyme.

Make it saucy!

These creamy mushrooms make a delicious pasta sauce. Add a splash of pasta cooking water to loosen the creamy mushrooms, then stir through the cooked pasta to serve.

Three ways with eggs

Eggs are awesome! All-in-one powerhouses of goodness, eggs make the perfect storecupboard staple. Best of all you can serve them up in so many different ways. Here are some ideas to add to your existing eggy repertoire.

serves 4 | prep 10 minutes | cook 5 minutes

Breakfast burritos

4 small **corn or wheat tortillas**

1 **avocado**, peeled, stoned and diced

Juice of ½ **lime**

55 g/2 oz **Cheddar cheese**, grated

30 g/1 oz **unsalted butter**

1 small **orange pepper**, deseeded and chopped

4 **spring onions**, sliced

1 **courgette**, grated

½–1 teaspoon **fajita spice mix** (optional)

6 **eggs**, lightly beaten

2 handfuls of **rocket** leaves

Preheat the oven to 140°C/275°F/Gas Mark 1. Wrap the tortillas in foil and put them in the oven to warm up.

Put the avocado in a bowl and pour over the lime juice. Put the cheese in a separate bowl.

Melt the butter in a non-stick saucepan over a gentle heat. Add the pepper, spring onions and courgette and sauté for 2 minutes until softened.

Beat the spice mix, if using, into the eggs, then pour them into the pan. Stir and turn the eggs over a gentle heat until scrambled, making sure they don't stick to the base of the pan.

Place each tortilla on a serving plate and top with some scrambled egg mixture. Let everyone help themselves to the avocado, cheese and rocket. Tuck in just like that, or roll up your tortilla to enclose the filling.

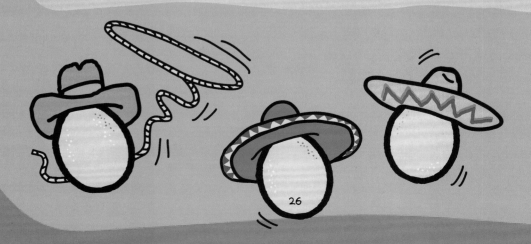

Herb, feta + quinoa frittata

serves 4–6 | prep 10 minutes | cook 20 minutes | 10+

30 g/1 oz **quinoa** (or 90 g/3¼ oz **ready-cooked quinoa**)

1 tablespoon **olive oil**

6 **spring onions**, chopped

6 **eggs**

1 teaspoon **dried oregano**

5 **sun-dried tomatoes** in oil, drained and chopped

100 g/3½ oz **feta cheese**, crumbled

20 g/¾ oz **unsalted butter**

Freshly ground **black pepper**

Grilled **baby tomatoes**, to serve

If you're cooking the quinoa, cover it with water in a pan, bring to the boil over a medium heat, then reduce the heat and simmer for 12 minutes, or until tender. Drain well and leave in the sieve. Meanwhile, heat the oil in a frying pan over a medium–low heat, and fry the spring onions for 3 minutes until softened. Lightly beat the eggs in a bowl and stir in the quinoa, the spring onions, oregano, tomatoes and feta. Season with pepper.

Preheat the grill to medium. Melt the butter in the frying pan, and add the egg mixture. Cook for 4–5 minutes until the base is set. Put the pan under the grill for 2–3 minutes to set the top. Turn out, cut into wedges and serve with grilled tomatoes.

Poached eggs with avocado hollandaise

serves 4–6 | prep 10 minutes | cook 5 minutes

4 large handfuls of **baby spinach leaves**

4 large **eggs**

A splash of **vinegar**

4 **wholemeal muffins**, split in half and toasted

For the avocado hollandaise

1 **avocado**, halved, stoned and flesh scooped out

2 tablespoons **mayonnaise**

1 tablespoon **natural yogurt**

2 teaspoons **lemon juice**

½ teaspoon **Dijon mustard**

To make the hollandaise, using a hand blender, blitz together all the ingredients with 2 tablespoons of water until smooth. Set aside.

Put the spinach in a heatproof bowl, cover with just-boiled water and leave to soften.

To poach the eggs, half-fill a saucepan with just-boiled water and stand the pan over a low heat. Swirl the water, then add a splash of vinegar. Crack 1 egg into a small bowl, then slip it into the water. Repeat for the other eggs. Poach the eggs for 4 minutes, making sure the water simmers but doesn't boil. Remove each egg with a slotted spoon and drain on kitchen paper. Lay two muffin halves side by side and top with drained spinach, an egg and a spoonful of the hollandaise. (Half a muffin may be enough for little ones.)

Lucky dip crispy mix

serves 6–8 | prep 5 minutes | cook 10 minutes

This fruity, nutty delicious muesli makes a hearty breakfast for grown-ups. The crunchy crispies in the mix mean that it's a muesli that little ones will love, too.

What you need

70 g/2½ oz **pecan nuts**

70 g/2½ oz **blanched almonds**

70 g/2½ oz **sunflower seeds**

100 g/3½ oz **wholegrain no-sugar rice crispies**

40 g/1½ oz **dried apple slices**, chopped

70 g/2½ oz ready-to-eat **dried dates**, roughly chopped

Whole milk and **fresh fruit**, to serve

What to do

1. Put the pecans and almonds in a large, dry frying pan over a medium–low heat and toast for 4 minutes, turning once, until starting to colour, then tip them out of the pan onto a plate. Add the sunflower seeds to the pan and repeat, toasting them for 3 minutes, shaking the pan occasionally. Repeat with the rice crispies, toasting them for 2 minutes. Leave the seeds, nuts and crispies to cool.

2. When everything is cool, chop the nuts, then tip them into a large bowl and add the seeds and crispies. Add the apple slices and dates, then stir until combined. If serving to small children, make sure everything is finely chopped.

3. Serve the muesli in bowls with milk, topped with fresh fruit. Store any remaining muesli in an airtight jar for up to 10 days.

Find the crispies!

Sugar-free rice crispies are usually stocked in the gluten-free food aisles at supermarkets.

Topped tattie wedges

serves 4 | prep 5 minutes | cook 10 minutes | freeze me (cooked or uncooked)

Crispy potato scone wedges with a selection of favourite toppings give everyone a chance to choose their perfect breakfast or brunch. Make sure there's some left for the chef, too!

What you need

400 g/14 oz **cooked potato**, mashed

40 g/1½ oz **unsalted butter**, melted, plus extra for cooking

85 g/3 oz **plain flour**, plus extra for dusting

1 teaspoon **dried oregano** (optional)

To serve, choose from:

Fried, poached or scrambled **eggs**

Cooked **spinach**

Grilled **tomatoes**

Fried **mushrooms**

Special Baked Beans (see page 51)

Mashed or sliced **avocado**

What to do

1. Put the potato in a bowl with the melted butter, flour and oregano, if using, and beat to a smooth, stiff dough. Shape into a ball.

2. Roll out the dough on a lightly floured work surface until about 5 mm/¼ inch thick. Use a 23-cm/9-in plate as a template to cut the dough into a round.

3. Over a medium heat, melt enough butter to lightly coat the base of a large frying pan. Using a spatula, transfer the potato cake to the pan, prick the top with a fork and cook for 3–4 minutes on each side until light golden and crisp. (To turn the potato scone, place a large plate on top of the pan and carefully flip it over, then slip the scone back into the pan, uncooked-side down.) Serve the potato scone cut into wedges with your favourite topping.

Spinach makes me strong!

Can I help?

Roll up, roll up!

There are lots of ways little ones can get involved with this yummy brunch. They can roll out the dough, and then (with help, as necessary) carefully cut around the plate to make the perfect dough circle. Talking about shapes is learning while cooking, too!

Slurp-me-up smoothies

The green one

 serves 4 prep 5 minutes freeze me

325 g/11½ oz cored **pineapple**, cut into chunks

1 small **avocado**, peeled, stoned and cut into chunks

2 **bananas**, sliced

2 handfuls of **baby spinach leaves**, tough stalks removed

450 ml/¾ pint **coconut drinking milk**

Blend all the ingredients together until smooth and creamy. Serve immediately.

If you like, you can freeze this smoothie to make a delicious, creamy ice.

The orange one

 serves 4 prep 5 minutes freeze me
+ soaking

70 g/2½ oz unsulphured ready-to-eat **dried apricots**

Juice of 8 **oranges**

Juice of 1 small **lemon**

1 **carrot**, peeled and coarsely grated

Put the apricots in a bowl, cover with 125 ml/4 fl oz warm water and soak for 30 minutes, or overnight. Blend the apricots and soaking water with the orange and lemon juices and the carrot, until smooth. Serve immediately.

If you like, you can freeze this smoothie to make a delicious granita.

The purple one

 serves 4 prep 5 minutes freeze me

300 g/10½ oz **strawberries**, hulled

40 g/1½ oz **porridge oats**

150 g/5½ oz **blueberries** or **raspberries**

1 teaspoon **ground cinnamon**

1 teaspoon **vanilla extract**

300 ml/½ pint **whole milk**

200 ml/7 fl oz **natural yogurt**

Blend all the ingredients together until smooth and creamy. Serve immediately.

If you like, you can freeze this smoothie to make a delicious yogurt ice.

The red one

 serves 4 prep 5 minutes freeze me

100 g/3½ oz **cooked beetroot** (not in vinegar)

200 g/7 oz **frozen stoned cherries**

1-cm/½-inch piece of **root ginger**, peeled and grated

450 ml/¾ pint **fresh apple juice** (not from concentrate)

Finely grated rind of 1 **orange**

Put all the ingredients in a blender and blend until smooth. Serve immediately.

If you like, you can freeze this smoothie to make a delicious granita.

Brilliant breakfast cake

This cake is packed with healthy orange, cherries, carrots, nuts and natural yogurt. It's a cake to keep everyone happy! You can store it in an airtight container for up to three days.

What you need

Unsalted butter, for greasing

250 g/9 oz **wholemeal self-raising flour**

1 teaspoon **baking powder**

2 teaspoons **ground cinnamon**

2 teaspoons **mixed spice**

100 ml/3½ fl oz **sunflower oil**

100 ml/3½ fl oz **natural yogurt**

3 **eggs**, lightly beaten

175 ml/6 fl oz **clear honey**, plus extra for drizzling

Finely grated rind of 1 **orange** and 4 tablespoons juice

55 g/2 oz **walnuts**, chopped

250 g/9 oz **carrots**, peeled, coarsely grated and patted dry

55 g/2 oz **sour cherries** or **raisins**, chopped if large

2 tablespoons **natural yogurt** and 2–3 peeled **orange** slices (white pith removed) per cake square, to serve

What to do

1. Preheat the oven to 180°C/350°F/Gas Mark 4. Lightly grease and line a 23-cm/9-in square brownie tin.

2. Sift together the flour, baking powder, cinnamon and mixed spice in a large bowl.

3. Beat together the oil, yogurt, eggs, honey, orange rind and juice, then stir this mixture into the dry ingredients. Gently fold in the walnuts, carrots and sour cherries or raisins, then pour the mixture into the prepared tin and level the top.

4. Bake for 35–40 minutes, until risen and cooked through. Leave to cool in the tin for 5 minutes, then turn out and cut into 12 squares. Serve warm or cold topped with yogurt, orange slices and a drizzle of honey.

Purple-topped potato + parsnip cakes

Add a splash of colour to breakfast with these fritters. They're yummy on their own, but much prettier (and more delicious) with the beetroot and smoked salmon topping.

What you need

300 g/10½ oz white **potatoes**, peeled and coarsely grated or spiralized

125 g/4½ oz **parsnip**, peeled and coarsely grated or spiralized

2½ tablespoons **plain flour**

¾ teaspoon **baking powder**

1 **egg**, lightly beaten

Sunflower oil, for frying

4 slices of **smoked salmon**, cut into strips, to serve (optional)

For the topping

4 tablespoons **crème fraîche**

1 tablespoon juice and ½ teaspoon finely grated rind of 1 **lemon**

1 teaspoon **horseradish sauce** (optional)

1 **cooked beetroot** (not in vinegar), grated (optional)

Brrr... freezing!

To freeze the parsnip cakes, leave them to cool, then spread them out on a greaseproof-lined baking tray and open-freeze until hard. When frozen, layer them in greaseproof paper and pack them in a freezer bag.

What to do

1. Put the prepared potatoes and parsnip into a clean tea towel, gather up the sides into a bundle and squeeze over a sink to extract as much water from the vegetables as possible. Put the vegetables into a large bowl with the flour, baking powder and egg, then mix together until combined.

2. To make the topping, mix together all the topping ingredients until combined – you could leave out the horseradish sauce for young children or serve the beetroot separately, if you prefer. Leave to one side.

3. Over a medium heat, heat enough oil to cover the base of a large frying pan. Take a small handful of the mixture (about one-eighth), allowing any excess egg to drip off, and place it in the pan. Flatten the top to make a thin fritter, then repeat to cook four fritters at a time. Cook for 3 minutes on each side, or until light golden and crisp.

4. Line an ovenproof plate with kitchen paper. When the fritters are cooked, lift them out of the frying pan onto the plate and keep them warm in a low oven. Repeat steps 3 and 4 until you have 8 parsnip cakes in total.

5. Serve the parsnip cakes topped with the crème fraîche mixture and a few strips of smoked salmon, if using – bearing in mind that smoked salmon is quite salty so go easy on it for children, or leave it out altogether.

Good-morning muesli bread

makes
1
loaf
prep
10 minutes
cook
50 minutes
freeze me

What better sunshine-y start to the day than with a special bread made of muesli and yogurt. Pressing the dough is a good way to get those muscles working in the morning, too!

What you need

Sunflower oil, for greasing

400 g/14 oz **wholemeal plain flour** (or 50:50 white and wholemeal), plus extra for dusting

70 g/2½ oz **sugar-free muesli**

2 teaspoons **mixed spice**

1 teaspoon **bicarbonate of soda**

1 teaspoon **salt**

115 g/4 oz **dried figs**, chopped into chunks, or **raisins**

300–350 ml/10–12 fl oz **natural yogurt**

1 tablespoon **lemon** juice

1 tablespoon **clear honey**

What to do

1. Preheat the oven to 200°C/400°F/Gas Mark 6. Lightly grease a large baking sheet with oil.

2. Mix the flour, muesli, mixed spice, bicarbonate of soda and salt in a large bowl. Stir in the figs or raisins, then make a well in the centre. Mix together the smaller amount of yogurt with the lemon juice and honey and pour the mixture into the dry ingredients. Stir with a fork and then mix with your hands to make a soft, sticky dough, adding more yogurt if needed. (Don't work the dough for too long as that will result in a heavy loaf.)

3. Tip the dough out onto a floured work surface and form into a round, then flatten the top until the dough is about 4 cm/1½ in thick.

4. Place the dough on the prepared baking sheet and sift over a little extra flour. Cut a deep cross through the dough almost to the bottom, then bake for 45–50 minutes, or until risen and the loaf sounds hollow when tapped underneath. Transfer to a wire rack to cool. Serve in slices. The bread will keep in an airtight container for up to three days.

Make me a baker!

Can I help?

This loaf is so super-quick and easy to make it's perfect for little hands who want to have a go at kneading.

Hola! Spanish potatoes

serves 4 | prep 10 minutes | cook 40 minutes | freeze me (sauce only)

Bursting with smoky Spanish flavours, these tapas-style potatoes are made for sharing. Snap your fingers, clap your hands and call 'Almuerzo!' – lunch!

What you need

600 g/1 lb 5 oz **floury potatoes**, such as Maris Piper, cut into small chunks

1 tablespoon **olive oil**

85 g/3 oz **chorizo sausage**, skin removed and diced

1 **onion**, chopped

1 small **red pepper**, deseeded and finely chopped

2 large **garlic** cloves, chopped

400 g/14 oz **passata**

1 tablespoon **tomato purée**

½–1 teaspoon **sweet smoked paprika**

1 teaspoon chopped **thyme**

4 **eggs**

Dried chilli flakes, for sprinkling (optional)

What to do

1. Preheat the oven to 220°C/425°F/Gas Mark 7. Toss the potatoes in the oil, tip them into a large roasting tin, and spread them out into an even layer. Roast for 35–40 minutes, turning them halfway, until golden and crisp.

2. Meanwhile, heat a large, dry frying pan over a medium heat. Add the chorizo and cook for 4 minutes, stirring frequently, or until the chorizo releases its oil and turns crisp. Remove the chorizo with a slotted spoon, leaving the oil in the pan, and add the onion and red pepper. Reduce the heat to medium–low and cook for 5 minutes, or until softened.

3. Stir in the garlic, then add the passata, tomato purée, smoked paprika and thyme and simmer for 10 minutes until thickened, adding a splash of water if it becomes too dry.

4. Meanwhile, hard-boil the eggs, refresh under cold running water, then peel and quarter.

5. To serve, spoon the potatoes onto plates, top with the sauce, hard-boiled eggs, chorizo, and chilli flakes, if using. The sauce will keep in an airtight container for up to 3 days.

From 10 months

For babies

Replace the chorizo with a small amount of unsmoked ham or lean unsmoked bacon to reduce salt and fat; chop or coarsely mash the potatoes and eggs after cooking and mix them into the tomato mixture.

Hearty red chicken soup

serves 4 · prep 10 minutes · cook 30 minutes · freeze me (soup only)

This is a big bowl of colourful wonderfulness! With crunchy sweetcorn, fill-me-up beans and a sprinkle of fajita spice, this extra-special chicken soup will satisfy your bellies, warm your toes and delight your taste buds.

What you need

1 tablespoon **olive oil**, plus extra for brushing

1 **onion**, finely chopped

1 **carrot**, peeled and diced

2 large **garlic** cloves, finely chopped

1 **red pepper**, deseeded and chopped

400 g/14 oz **passata**

500 ml/17 fl oz reduced-salt **chicken stock**

210 g/7½ oz can **kidney beans** in water, drained

½–1 teaspoon **fajita spice mix** (optional)

1 teaspoon **dried oregano**

250 g/9 oz skinless, boneless **chicken breasts**, cut into large bite-sized pieces

115 g/4 oz no-sugar, no-salt canned **sweetcorn**, drained, or kernels stripped from 1 cob

2 soft **corn tortillas**

What to do

1. Heat the oil in a large saucepan over a medium–low heat. Add the onion, carrot, garlic and red pepper, cover with a lid and cook for 10 minutes, stirring occasionally, until softened.

2. Preheat the oven to 180°C/350°F/Gas Mark 4. Add the passata, stock, beans, fajita spice mix, if using, and oregano to the pan and bring the mixture up to the boil. Reduce the heat to low, part-cover with a lid and simmer for 10 minutes.

3. Stir the chicken into the pan and cook for another 7 minutes, or until the chicken is cooked through, then add the sweetcorn and heat until the corn is warm and tender.

4. While the soup is cooking, make the tortilla chips. Brush both sides of each tortilla with olive oil, then cut into thin strips. Put the strips on a baking sheet and bake for 5–7 minutes, turning once, or until crisp. Transfer to a wire rack to cool. To serve, ladle the soup into bowls with the corn chips on the side.

For babies

From 10 months

Blend the soup with a hand blender, adding a splash of water if it's too thick. Slurrrp!

45

Deep South salmon + wedges

Potato wedges, mildly flavoured with Cajun spices from the American Deep South and with stretchy cheese on top, are irresistible picking food for little fingers (and for big ones, too).

What you need

2 tablespoons **olive oil**, plus extra for greasing

2 teaspoons **Cajun spice mix** (optional)

600 g/1 lb 5 oz floury **potatoes**, such as Maris Piper, cut into chunky wedges

1 large **red pepper**, deseeded and cut into chunks

3 **spring onions**, sliced

125 g/4½ oz no-sugar, no-salt canned **sweetcorn**, well drained

225 g/8 oz can **red salmon**, drained, skin and bones removed, flaked

50 g/1¾ oz **mozzarella cheese**, grated

Dill, for sprinkling (optional)

Natural yogurt, to serve (optional)

Green salad, to serve

For the sweet chilli mayo dip (optional)

2 tablespoons **mayonnaise**

2 tablespoons **natural yogurt**

1 tablespoon **sweet chilli sauce**

What to do

1. Preheat the oven to 200°C/400°F/Gas Mark 6. Lightly grease a large roasting tin.

2. Mix together the oil and the spice mix, if using, in a large bowl. Add the potatoes and turn them in the spiced oil until coated, then tip them into the roasting tin. Spread them out evenly and roast for 20 minutes.

3. Meanwhile, put the red pepper and spring onions in the bowl with the spiced oil and turn to coat. Add a splash more oil, if needed.

4. Remove the roasting tin from the oven, turn the potatoes and scatter over the red pepper and spring onions. Return the tin to the oven for another 15 minutes. Mix the ingredients for the sweet chilli mayo dip, if serving.

5. Preheat the grill to medium–high. Remove the roasting tin from the oven and scatter the sweetcorn, salmon and cheese over the potato mixture. Grill for 5 minutes, or until the cheese melts. Serve the wedges with the sweet chilli mayo or natural yogurt, if using, sprinkled with a little dill, if you like, and a salad on the side.

From 10 months

Leave out the Cajun spice mix, then chop or coarsely mash everything once cooked and serve without the mayo.

For babies

Bubbly green soup

serves **4** prep **5** minutes cook **20** minutes freeze me (soup only)

Bubble, bubble, toil and trouble… This pea and leek soup is ready quick-as-a-flash! Take a bag of frozen peas and a few other storecupboard ingredients and everyone can tuck into a bowl of green goodness in no time at all. Little helpers can cast a spell as you stir!

What you need

1 tablespoon **olive oil**

1 **celery** stick, with leaves if any, thinly sliced

2 large **leeks**, trimmed and sliced

2 large **potatoes**, peeled and cubed

2 **bay leaves**

1 litre/1¾ pints reduced-salt **vegetable stock**

2 tablespoons **pumpkin seeds**, for sprinkling (optional)

400 g/14 oz **frozen peas**

For the minty yogurt

4 tablespoons **thick natural yogurt**

1 tablespoon chopped **mint** leaves

What to do

1. Heat the oil in a saucepan over a medium heat. Add the celery and leeks and cook for 4 minutes, stirring occasionally, until softened. Stir in the potatoes and bay leaves and sauté for a couple of minutes.

2. Pour in the stock. Bring to the boil, then lower the heat, part-cover with a lid and simmer for 10 minutes, until the potatoes are tender.

3. While the soup is cooking, toast the pumpkin seeds in a large, dry frying pan for 3 minutes until starting to colour – take care as they can pop! Also, make the minty yogurt by stirring together the yogurt and mint.

4. Add the peas to the soup and cook for 3 minutes, or until tender. Using a hand blender, blend the soup until thick and smooth, adding more stock or water, if needed. Serve in bowls, topped with a spoonful of the minty yogurt and a sprinkling of pumpkin seeds, if using.

Fizzy potion!

Just for fun

It's easy to make a magic potion with a few household ingredients. Fill a jam jar halfway with vinegar, then add a few drops of food colouring and maybe some glitter. Squeeze in some washing-up liquid, stir, and place the jar on a tray. Now add in a heaped teaspoon of baking soda, stir again, and watch the magic begin!

Four ways with easy toast toppers

Toast with tasty toppings makes such a quick and easy lunch for everyone. Cut the prepared toasty slices into fingers for little ones over 12 months.

Cauliflower cheese fingers

serves 4 | prep 5 minutes | cook 10 minutes

4 slices of **wholemeal bread**

2 **egg yolks**

¼ teaspoon **English mustard**

3 tablespoons **whole milk**

70 g/2½ oz **Cheddar cheese**, grated

4 **cauliflower florets**, grated

Unsalted butter, for spreading

Preheat the grill to medium–high. Lightly toast one side of each slice of bread. Meanwhile, mix together the egg yolks, mustard and milk in a bowl, then stir in the grated cheese and cauliflower.

Remove the toast from the grill and butter the untoasted side. Spoon the cheese mixture on top, spreading it out almost to the edges. Return to the grill for 5 minutes, or until the topping starts to turn golden. Leave to cool slightly before serving.

Sardine + red pesto toasts

serves 4 | prep 5 minutes | cook 5 minutes

4 slices of **wholemeal bread**

2 x 125 g/4½ oz cans **sardines** in oil, drained

4 teaspoons **sun-dried tomato pesto**

2 **spring onions**, finely chopped

2 **tomatoes**, deseeded and diced

Freshly ground **black pepper**

Preheat the grill to medium–high. Lightly toast one side of each slice of bread (about 2 minutes). Meanwhile, scoop the sardines from the cans, discarding the oil. Open them out and remove the spines. Put the sardines in a bowl and mash with the pesto, spring onions and tomatoes. Season with a little pepper.

Remove the toasts from the grill and spoon the sardine mixture onto the untoasted side of each slice of bread, spreading it out in an even layer almost to the edges. Return the toasts to the grill and cook for 3 minutes, or until the topping has heated through. Leave to cool slightly before serving.

Special baked beans on toast

serves 4 | prep 5 minutes | cook 15 minutes | freeze me (beans only)

1 tablespoon **olive oil**

1 **onion**, finely chopped

1 **celery** stick, finely chopped

400 g/14 oz can **haricot beans**, drained

1 heaped tablespoon **tomato purée**

2 teaspoons reduced-salt **soy sauce**

1 teaspoon **balsamic vinegar**

2 tablespoons **hummus**

4 slices **wholemeal bread**, toasted

Sweet chilli sauce, to serve (optional)

Heat the oil in a saucepan over a medium heat. Add the onion and celery, cover and cook for 5 minutes, stirring occasionally, until softened. Add the beans, tomato purée, soy sauce, vinegar and 3 tablespoons of water to the pan, stir until combined, then bring almost to the boil. Reduce the heat to low, cover with a lid and simmer for 8–10 minutes until the beans have softened.

Spread the hummus over the toast and top with the beans. For adult servings, add a splash of sweet chilli sauce, if using.

Smashed avocado toasts with sticky tomatoes

serves 4 | prep 5 minutes | cook 5 minutes

1 tablespoon **olive oil**

12 **baby plum tomatoes**, quartered

½–1 teaspoon **balsamic vinegar**

2 small ripe **avocados**, halved, stoned and flesh scooped out

Juice of ½ **lime**

4 slices of **light rye bread**, toasted

Freshly ground **black pepper**

A handful of small **basil** leaves (optional), to serve

Heat the oil in a large frying pan over a medium–low heat. Add the tomatoes and cook for 2 minutes, turning once, until softened. Stir in the balsamic vinegar and remove from the heat.

Mash the avocado with the lime juice and season with pepper. Spoon the avocado on top of the toasts, spreading it out in an even layer, top with the tomatoes and any juices in the pan. Season with a little black pepper and scatter over a few basil leaves just before serving, if using.

Fill-you-up tomato + lentil soup

serves **4** prep **10** minutes cook **30** minutes freeze me

This tomato soup is packed with nutritious lentils (which contain lots of protein and fibre) to make a satisfying lunch. Feta cheese adds smooth creaminess to every mouthful.

What you need

1 tablespoon **olive oil**, plus extra for drizzling

1 **onion**, chopped

1 **carrot**, peeled and grated

1 **celery** stick, chopped

1 **bay leaf**

1 teaspoon **dried thyme**

70 g/2½ oz **split red lentils**

600 ml/1 pint reduced-salt **vegetable stock**

400 g/14 oz **passata**

2 tablespoons **crème fraîche**

60 g/2¼ oz **feta cheese**, crumbled, to serve

For the garlic toasts

4 thick slices of **crusty wholemeal bread**

2 **garlic** cloves, halved

What to do

1. Heat the oil in a saucepan over a medium–low heat. Add the onion, carrot and celery, cover with a lid and cook for 6 minutes, stirring occasionally, until tender.

2. Stir in the bay leaf, thyme and lentils, then the stock and passata. Bring to the boil, then reduce the heat, cover and simmer for 20 minutes, or until reduced and thickened. Remove the bay leaf from the soup, then using a hand blender, blend the soup until smooth.

3. Meanwhile, make the garlic toasts. Heat a griddle pan over a high heat or preheat the grill to high. Toast the bread, turning once, until crisp and golden. Rub one side of each toast with garlic and drizzle over olive oil.

4. Stir the crème fraîche into the soup and warm through. Serve sprinkled with feta, with the garlic toasts on the side.

Learning with lentils

Just for fun

Red lentils are not only a fun colour, they make a brilliant noise when you pour them and they're dry so it doesn't matter if they end up on the floor! Find lots of different-sized kitchen containers, then let your little ones pour in some dried lentils and practise some weighing and pouring skills.

Rainbow lamb + couscous salad

serves 4 | prep 15 minutes | cook 15 minutes

All the colours in this scrummy salad are a sure sign that it is popping with vital nutrients. It's a great way to use up any leftover lamb, too!

What you need

60 g/2¼ oz **couscous**

4 tablespoons **flaked almonds** (optional)

1 tablespoon **olive oil**

1 **onion**, finely chopped

2 **carrots**, peeled and cut into ribbons or coarsely grated

1 **courgette**, cut into ribbons or coarsely grated

175 g/6 oz **leftover roast lamb** (or other roast meat), cut into thin strips

4 **radishes**, thinly sliced

6 ready-to-eat **dried dates**, roughly chopped

A handful of chopped **mint**

A handful of chopped **coriander**

For the dressing

3 tablespoons **extra virgin olive oil**

Finely grated rind and juice of 1 **lemon**

1 **garlic** clove, crushed

1 teaspoon **cumin seeds** (optional)

What to do

1. Put the couscous in a bowl, pour in just-boiled water to cover, put a plate on top and leave for 5 minutes to absorb the water and until the grains are tender. Fluff up with a fork.

2. Meanwhile, mix together all the ingredients for the dressing, adding the cumin seeds, if using, and set aside.

3. Toast the almonds, if using, in a large, dry frying pan for 2 minutes, or until starting to turn golden. Chop finely for young children. Heat a splash of oil in the frying pan over a medium heat. Add the onion and fry for 5 minutes, until soft. Stir in the carrots, courgette and lamb and heat for 5 minutes.

4. Tip into the bowl with the couscous, add the radishes, dates and herbs and combine gently. Pour over the dressing and combine again. Sprinkle with the almonds, if using, and serve warm or at room temperature.

Just for fun

Grow your own

Radishes take just 4 weeks to grow, making them perfect for budding gardeners who might be impatient to harvest their crop! Grow radishes outside in a tub during spring and summer, or in a box on a sunny windowsill all year round, then pick them, slice them and put them in your salad!

Dragon omelette rolls

serves 4 | prep 10 minutes | cook 10 minutes

Fresh and lively Chinese flavours give any leftover roast meat a new lease of life. Wrap it all up in a delicious eggy roll and then gobble it up quickly before that naughty dragon gets it...

What you need

1 tablespoon **sesame oil**

3 **spring onions**, cut into thin strips

1 **carrot**, peeled and cut into thin strips

½ **yellow pepper**, deseeded and cut into thin strips

2 handfuls of **kale** or **spinach**, tough stalks removed, leaves chopped

100 g/3½ oz **leftover roast meat**, such as pork, chicken or beef, cut into thin strips

1 teaspoon grated fresh **ginger root**, skin removed (optional)

30 g/1 oz **unsalted butter**

6 **eggs**

1 teaspoon reduced-salt **soy sauce**

What to do

1. Heat the sesame oil in a large frying pan over a medium heat. Add the spring onions, carrot, pepper, kale or spinach, roast meat and ginger, if using, and cook for 3 minutes, until just tender. Spoon into a bowl and set aside.

2. Add a third of the butter to the frying pan over a medium heat. Lightly beat 2 of the eggs, pour them into the pan and swirl it around until the eggs coat the base. Cook for a few minutes until set, then turn out onto a plate.

3. Spoon a third of the vegetables down one side of the omelette, add a splash of soy sauce (leave this out if serving to young children), roll it up into a cylinder and carefully cut in half crossways. Serve straightaway or keep warm in a low oven while you make 2 more omelette rolls.

Just for fun

Make your own dragon

You can make a fire-breathing dragon all of your own with an empty toilet roll wrapped in green or red paper. Draw on some eyes (or use stick on googly ones), then tape strips of yellow and red tissue paper to the inside of one end of the tube. Now blow the other end and watch your dragon breathe fire!

Moon + star flatbread pizza

serves 2-4 | prep 5 minutes | cook 20 minutes | freeze me (uncooked base only)

This is pizza with a Turkish twist (in fact, it's called a *pide* – pronounced pee-day – in Turkey). We've used minced beef for our recipe, but lamb or veggie mince is delicious, too. A *pide* is just perfect for sharing with a pal!

What you need

1 tablespoon **olive oil**, plus extra for brushing

1 **onion**, finely chopped

125 g/4½ oz lean **minced beef**

1 teaspoon **ground coriander**

¼ teaspoon **ground cinnamon**

2 **garlic** cloves, finely chopped

2 unsulphured ready-to-eat **dried apricots**, cut into small pieces

1 large round **flatbread**

2 **tomatoes**, deseeded and diced

50 g/1¾ oz **feta cheese**

½ teaspoon toasted **sesame seeds** (optional)

1 large handful of **rocket leaves** (optional)

What to do

1. Preheat the grill to high. Heat the oil in a large frying pan over a medium heat. Add the onion and beef, breaking up the mince with a spatula. Cook for 10 minutes, stirring often, until the onions are tender and the mince starts to turn crisp. Stir in the coriander, cinnamon, garlic and apricots and remove the pan from the heat.

2. Brush the top of the flatbread with oil and scatter over the mince mixture, followed by the tomatoes, feta and sesame seeds, if using. Place under the grill and cook for 5–8 minutes, or until the flatbread is crisp and the feta starts to colour. Remove from the grill, scatter over the rocket leaves, if using, and cut into wedges to serve.

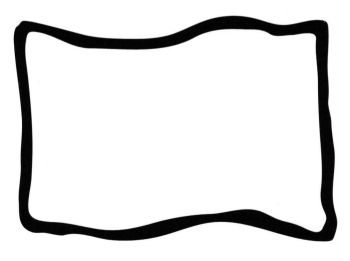

Design a special family flag here!

Make a keepsake tablecloth

We love the idea of a hand-decorated family tablecloth that you can keep for ever. If you prefer, though, you could use a paper tablecloth and crayons and make lots of versions for different occasions!

1

Gather your tools

Find a plain white tablecloth. You can use a large piece of cut white cotton or calico if you like (use fabric glue along the edges to stop them fraying). You'll also need some fabric pens, or permanent markers, and a plastic cloth to stop the pens marking the surface beneath. Finally, stencils or outlines are a great idea for really little ones who might need a hand with their drawing; and chalk will help you map out areas for design.

Have a practice

If you think artistic temperaments might cause wobbles, encourage everyone to plan their individual designs on paper first – that way family artists get to have a practice before they begin on the real thing. And, remember, the fun is in the freestyling!

60

② Plan your design

What theme do you want for your tablecloth? Knights and princesses, fairies, animals, even self-portraits are all good choices. Divide up the tablecloth allocating one section to each person who will be decorating. This way everyone gets their own place to be creative and you can all go at your own pace.

③ Get drawing!

It's time to begin. Probably on the floor is easiest, or on the table if you want to make sure the pictures will appear on the tabletop rather than on the hanging sides. Don't forget to put a protective layer underneath it though! When everyone's done (it may take a few sittings), make sure the cloth is dry and follow packet instructions to fix any fabric pens (some may need ironing). Voilà! A family masterpiece!

Party time!

This makes a great party activity. Using disposable tablecloths all your guests can decorate their own to take away for their family mealtimes at home.

61

Little monster chickpea stir-fry

Chickpeas are packed with nutrients that help support immunity and this stir-fry, with tuna and oozy cheese, is a great way to introduce them to little ones – and to little monsters, too!

What you need

2 tablespoons **olive oil**

2 **leeks**, trimmed and sliced

1 **orange pepper**, deseeded and diced

4 handfuls of **baby spinach leaves**, roughly chopped

400 g/14 oz can **chickpeas**, drained

1 **garlic** clove, finely chopped

1 teaspoon **dried oregano**

Juice of ½ **lemon**

½ teaspoon **Dijon mustard** (optional)

200 g/7 oz can **tuna chunks** in spring water, drained

125 g/4½ oz **mozzarella cheese**, drained, patted dry and torn into chunks

Crusty wholemeal bread, to serve

What to do

1. Heat the oil in a large frying pan or wok set over a medium heat. Add the leeks and orange pepper and stir-fry for 4 minutes until softened.

2. Add the spinach, chickpeas, garlic and oregano and stir-fry for 3 minutes until the spinach has wilted.

3. Reduce the heat to medium–low and add the lemon juice, mustard, if using, tuna and mozzarella cheese and cook for 2 minutes until the cheese melts slightly and turns gooey. Serve with crusty bread on the side.

Try it this way!

Instead of the chickpeas, try using fresh gnocchi. Add the gnocchi to the pan with the spinach, garlic and oregano and stir-fry until golden.

Dunkable cheesy broccoli fritters

These broccoli fritters are the perfect shape for dunking in a zingy red-pepper sauce. They also make great rest stops for naughty toy frogs!

What you need

Olive oil, for greasing

375 g/13 oz **broccoli florets**

4 **spring onions**, finely chopped

150 g/5½ oz **mature Cheddar cheese**, grated

90 g/3¼ oz **wholemeal breadcrumbs**

3 **eggs**, lightly beaten

Potato wedges and **salad**, to serve

For the red-pepper sauce

2 teaspoons **extra virgin olive oil**

1 large **red pepper**, deseeded and sliced

1 **garlic** clove, peeled

1 tablespoon **lemon** juice

1 teaspoon **paprika**

2 tablespoons **ground almonds**

What to do

1. Preheat the oven to 200°C/400°F/Gas Mark 6. Line two baking sheets with baking parchment and lightly grease with oil.

2. Steam the broccoli for 3 minutes until lightly cooked, then refresh under cold running water and drain well. Tip the broccoli onto a clean tea towel and pat dry.

3. Blitz the broccoli in a food processor until finely chopped, then place in a large bowl with the spring onions, cheese and breadcrumbs and stir well until combined. Make a dip in the centre of the broccoli mixture and add the eggs, then mix well until everything is combined.

4. Use your hands to form the mixture into 18 x 5-cm/7 × 2-in long fritters and place on the prepared baking sheets. Bake for 20–25 minutes until firm and starting to turn golden.

5. While the fritters are cooking, make the red pepper sauce. Put all the ingredients in a food processor or blender and blitz until almost smooth. Serve the sauce with the fritters, potato wedges and a salad.

Fritter fingers

Can I help?

Squidging the fritter mixture into shape is fantastic fun made for little hands!

Eye-spy eggs

Eggs peeking out from tomato-y sauce – yummy! These eggs are 'baked' on the hob, so they're really simple to make. Serve them with crusty bread – which is just right for dipping in the runny yolks and mopping up the tangy sauce.

What you need

1 tablespoon **olive oil**

4 **spring onions**, finely chopped

2 **garlic** cloves, finely chopped

1 teaspoon **ground cumin**

1 teaspoon mild **smoked paprika**

1 teaspoon **dried thyme**

400 g/14 oz can **chopped tomatoes**

4 **eggs**

2 tablespoons **coriander** leaves (optional)

Sprinkling of **dried chilli flakes** (optional)

Crusty wholemeal bread, to serve

What to do

1. Heat the oil in a frying pan with a tight-fitting lid over a medium heat. Add the spring onions and cook for 3 minutes until softened. Stir in the garlic, spices and thyme followed by the chopped tomatoes, then bring the sauce almost to the boil. Reduce the heat, part-cover with a lid and simmer for 5 minutes until the sauce has reduced and thickened.

2. Make 4 evenly spaced dips in the sauce using the back of a spoon. Crack an egg into each dip, cover the pan with a lid and cook gently for 10 minutes or until the egg whites are set but the yolks are still a little runny (see note for little ones).

3. Sprinkle the baked eggs with coriander, if using, and for adults a sprinkling of dried chilli flakes, if using, and serve with crusty bread on the side.

For babies

From 10 months

Make sure the eggs are cooked all the way through and then chop everything up to a perfect texture for your baby.

Build-it bean burgers

 serves **4**
 prep **15** minutes
 cook **20** minutes
 freeze me

+ soaking

(cooked or uncooked burger)

Our little helpers loved building and eating their own tasty meat-free burgers. Who can resist stacking up the lettuce and tomatoes and dolloping on the special sauce? You have to open *reeeally* wide to take a big bite!

What you need

Olive oil, for greasing and brushing

1½ x 400 g/14 oz cans **chickpeas**, well drained and patted dry

2 **garlic** cloves, peeled

3 **spring onions**, finely chopped

1 heaped tablespoon **pumpkin seeds**

A handful of **flat-leaf parsley** leaves

1 teaspoon **ground cumin**

½ teaspoon **bicarbonate of soda**

2 tablespoons **plain flour**

4 **wholemeal burger buns**, lightly toasted

Tahini Yogurt Sauce (see page 153) or **mayonnaise** and **mixed salad**, to serve

What to do

1. Preheat the oven to 180°C/350°F/Gas Mark 4 and grease a large baking sheet with oil.

2. Put the chickpeas, garlic, spring onions, pumpkin seeds, parsley and cumin in a food processor and blend to a coarse paste. You will occasionally have to push the mixture down from the sides of the processor to mix everything together evenly. Stir in the bicarbonate of soda and flour to make a thick, coarse paste – it will be slightly wet but will hold together when baked.

3. Using your hands, divide the chickpea mixture into four and shape each portion into a burger. Place on the prepared tray and brush each one with a little oil. Bake for 20 minutes, turning once, until firm and light golden in places. Place each burger in a bun with the Tahini Yogurt Sauce or a dollop of mayonnaise and your favourite salad veg.

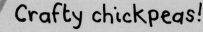

 For babies

From 10 months

Little ones can enjoy a bun-less burger, as long as it is chopped or mashed up well.

Crafty chickpeas!

Just for fun

Painting dried chickpeas is a brilliant way to help little ones develop their fine motor skills. Drain and empty the chickpeas from the can and leave them to dry (they dry very quickly), then get your little ones to dip them or use a brush to paint them different colours. They could be boulders for a toy digger, or poured into a plastic bottle to make a colourful music shaker.

Zesty prawn pasta salad

serves **4** prep **10** minutes cook **10** minutes

This recipe is made using orzo, a pasta shaped like big grains of rice. Orzo is a good size for little ones who are ready to chew, and adds substance to a salad for everybody. The juicy prawns and veggies dressed with zesty yogurt sizzle with summer flavours.

What you need

225 g/8 oz **orzo pasta**

115 g/4 oz **frozen peas**

2 tablespoons **extra virgin olive oil**

200 g/7 oz **cooked prawns**

2 **courgettes**, coarsely grated or spiralized

2 **garlic** cloves, finely chopped

225 g/8 oz **cherry tomatoes**, chopped

Finely grated rind and juice of ½ small **lemon**

2 large handfuls of **rocket** leaves

Lemon yogurt dressing (optional)

Finely grated rind and juice of ½ small **lemon**

3 tablespoons **natural yogurt**

What to do

1. Cook the orzo according to the packet instructions (about 8–9 minutes), adding the peas 3 minutes before the end of the cooking time. Drain and leave to one side.

2. Meanwhile, to make the lemon yogurt, if using, mix together the half lemon rind and juice with the yogurt. Set aside.

3. Heat the oil in a large frying pan over a medium heat. Add the prawns, courgettes, garlic and tomatoes and cook for 30 seconds, stirring. Add the half lemon rind and juice, and the pasta and peas and stir until combined and warmed through.

4. Divide the rocket among four shallow bowls and top with the orzo mixture. Drizzle over the lemon yogurt before serving. You may prefer to serve the orzo without the lemon yogurt to young children.

Get grating!

Can I help?

Ask any willing sous-chef to help you grate the courgettes. Just make sure you watch those little fingers!

Salsa-on-top sweet potato

Baked sweet potato has all the fluffiness of regular baked potato with added natural sweetness and extra nutrients (the ones that give veggies their vibrant colours). We've heaped salmon and a fruity salsa on top of ours – irresistible!

What you need

3–4 **sweet potatoes**, depending on their size

2 cooked skinless, boneless **salmon fillets**, flaked into pieces

For the pineapple salsa

200 g/7 oz cored **pineapple**, cut into small chunks

1 large **spring onion**, finely chopped

4 heaped tablespoons chopped **mint**

1 small **courgette**, coarsely grated

Juice of 1 **lime**

½ **red chilli**, deseeded and diced (optional)

What to do

1. Preheat the oven to 200°C/400°F/Gas Mark 6. Bake the sweet potatoes for 50 minutes, or until tender.

2. While the potatoes are cooking, mix together all the ingredients for the salsa. Adults may like to add the chilli to their portion.

3. To serve, slice through and open out the sweet potatoes. Flake the salmon over the top and finish with a large spoonful of the salsa.

For babies

From 10 months

Scoop out the flesh of the sweet potato and mash it down to the perfect texture with a little flaked salmon mixed in.

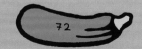

72

Surprise! Surprise! Cauliflower pizzette

The Italian word 'pizzette' means mini-pizzas, and our gluten-free mini-pizzas are super-special because we've used cauliflower to make the bases. Surprise!

What you need

Olive oil, for greasing and drizzling

90 g/3¼ oz **porridge oats**

1 **cauliflower**, cut into florets

100 g/3½ oz **ground almonds**

1 teaspoon **dried oregano**

2 **eggs**, lightly beaten

Your **favourite toppings**, such as slices of pepper and olive

125 g/4½ oz **mozzarella cheese**, drained, patted dry and torn into pieces

Freshly ground **black pepper**

Shavings of **Parmesan cheese** (optional), **basil leaves** and **mixed salad**, to serve

For the pizza sauce

200 g/7 oz **passata**

1 **garlic** clove, crushed

½ small **red pepper**, deseeded and sliced

1 tablespoon **tomato purée**

What to do

1. Preheat the oven to 220°C/425°F/Gas Mark 7. Line two large baking sheets with baking parchment and grease liberally with oil.

2. Process the oats to a powder in a food processor, then tip them into a bowl. Put the cauliflower in the processor and blitz until finely chopped to a crumb. Tip the cauliflower into the bowl with the oats and add the ground almonds, half the oregano and the eggs. Season with pepper and stir until combined – it will be fairly wet and crumbly but will hold together when baked.

3. Press the cauliflower mixture down into the bowl in an even layer. Scoop out a quarter of the mixture with your hands and press it into a round with raised edges, about 16 cm/6¼ in in diameter and 5 mm/¼ in thick on the lined baking sheet. Repeat with the remaining cauli mixture to make four pizza bases in total. Bake for 20 minutes, swapping the trays round halfway, until firm and golden.

4. While the bases are cooking, make the tomato sauce. Blend everything together with the remaining oregano until smooth. Spoon the sauce on top of the cooked pizza bases. Sprinkle over your choice of toppings, then the mozzarella cheese, then drizzle over a little olive oil. Bake for 10 minutes until the mozzarella melts. Serve topped with Parmesan shavings, if using, and basil leaves with a mixed salad on the side.

For babies

From 10 months

Sliced into wedges and topped with just cheese and tomato, pizzette make great finger food!

.75

Choo-choo! sushi

makes 20 | prep 15 minutes | cook 10 minutes
+ soaking
+ chilling

All aboard the sushi train! We love the idea of introducing little ones to world foods and these Japanese sushi are not only mega-delicious to eat together, but easy enough to *make* together, too!

What you need

325 g/11½ oz **sushi rice**

Juice of ½ large **lemon**

150 g/5½ oz **smoked trout or salmon**

1 tablespoon **horseradish sauce**

1 tablespoon **mayonnaise**

1½ **nori sheets**

Reduced-salt **soy sauce** and **pickled ginger** (optional), to serve

What to do

1. Put the rice in a bowl, cover with water and leave to soak for 30 minutes, then drain and rinse a couple of times. Transfer the rice to a saucepan, cover with 325 ml/11 fl oz of water and bring to the boil. Turn the heat to its lowest setting, cover with a lid and simmer for about 10 minutes, or until the water is absorbed and the rice is tender. Leave the rice to stand off the heat, covered, for 15 minutes.

2. Tip the rice onto a large platter and leave to cool, then stir in the lemon juice.

3. Line a 23-cm/9-in square baking tin with clingfilm, leaving enough overhanging to cover the top. Line the base of the tin with the trout or salmon, the slices slightly overlapping. Mix together the horseradish sauce and mayonnaise and smear over the fish in an even layer. Using a wet knife, spread the rice over the top in an even layer. Use scissors to cut the nori sheets to fit and finish with a layer of nori.

4. Fold the clingfilm over the top of the sushi, then gently but firmly press down and chill for 1 hour. Just before serving, lift the sushi out of the tin using the clingfilm to help, then, using a wet-bladed knife, cut into 20 pieces. Serve with small bowls of soy sauce and pickled ginger, if using.

76

Family feasts

Fruity lamb pilaf

serves 4 | prep 15 minutes | cook 30 minutes

A pilaf is a Middle Eastern rice dish that is cooked in a tasty broth. Our version uses warming spices and tangy apricots to add a comforting, fruity treat to every mouthful.

What you need

200 g/7 oz **brown basmati rice**

1 tablespoon **olive oil**

15 g/½ oz **unsalted butter**

2 **onions**, chopped

350 g/12 oz **lamb**, excess fat trimmed and meat diced

2 teaspoons **turmeric**

2 teaspoons **ground cumin**

1 teaspoon **ground allspice**

1 teaspoon **ground cinnamon**

70 g/2½ oz unsulphured ready-to-eat **dried apricots**, roughly chopped

2 **lemons**, halved

100 g/3½ oz **cauliflower**, grated

6 tablespoons **natural yogurt**

2 large handfuls of chopped **mint**

2 handfuls of finely chopped **pistachio nuts** (optional)

What to do

1. Put the rice in a bowl and cover with cold water. Leave to soak while you cook the onions. Heat the oil and butter in a large saucepan over a medium heat. Add the onions and cook for 5 minutes, or until softened. Add the lamb and cook for 5 minutes, turning until browned all over.

2. Drain the rice and rinse it under cold running water, then add to the pan with the spices, and stir. Add 400 ml/14 fl oz water and bring to the boil over a medium heat. Stir in the apricots and 2 of the lemon halves. Reduce the heat to low, cover with a lid and simmer for 15–20 minutes, or until the water has been absorbed and the rice is tender. Stir in the cauliflower and stand, covered, for 5 minutes.

3. While the rice is cooking, squeeze the remaining lemon halves into the yogurt and set aside.

4. Stir three-quarters of the mint into the rice, then spoon onto plates and top with the lamb, then the lemon yogurt, remaining mint, and a sprinkling of nuts, if using.

From 10 months

For babies

Leave out the pistachio nuts for babies, then chop or mash to the right texture.

Ella's shortcut

Replace the apricots with 1 x 70 g pouch of Ella's Kitchen peaches peaches peaches. It'll give you the same pleasing sweetness without the bits!

Wiggly chicken, cucumber + sugar snap noodles

Why is eating noodles so much fun? Twiddle them, slurp them, scoop them – everyone has their own favourite technique. With cucumber and sugar snap peas mixed in, this noodle dish is not only slurpy, it gives good crunch, too!

What you need

185 g/6½ oz **wholewheat noodles**

1 tablespoon **sunflower oil**

2 large **spring onions**, sliced diagonally, white and green parts separated

175 g/6 oz **cooked chicken**, shredded

85 g/3 oz **sugar snap peas**, sliced diagonally

6-cm/2½-in piece of **cucumber**, quartered lengthways, deseeded, and cut into chunks

2 **garlic** cloves, finely chopped

2.5-cm/1-in piece of fresh **root ginger**, peeled and finely chopped (optional)

2 **eggs**, lightly beaten

1 tablespoon reduced-salt **soy sauce**

A splash of **sesame oil**

Sweet chilli sauce (optional)

What to do

1) Cook the noodles in a saucepan of boiling water, following the packet instructions (about 5 minutes), until tender.

2) Meanwhile, heat a large wok over a high heat. Add the oil, the white spring onions, the chicken, sugar snap peas, cucumber, garlic and ginger, if using, and stir-fry for 2 minutes until the chicken is heated through and the vegetables just tender.

3) Make a well in the centre, pour in the eggs and stir until the eggs start to cook and scramble (about 3 minutes), then mix them into the rest of the ingredients in the wok.

4) Drain the noodles, reserving 3 tablespoons of the cooking water and add them both to the wok with the soy sauce and sesame oil. Turn briefly until everything is combined and then serve in bowls, sprinkled with the green part of the spring onions and with sweet chilli sauce for the grown-ups, if using.

From 10 months

For babies

Soy sauce is a bit too salty for little ones, so leave it out. Then, chop up the dish to your baby's usual texture.

Eastern chicken pan-fry

serves 4 · prep 10 minutes · cook 20 minutes · freeze me

+ marinating

Inspire the whole family to love the flavours of the East with this special chicken stir-fry. It combines familiar foods with exotic spices – and kale for an extra hit of goodness!

What you need

1 tablespoon reduced-salt **soy sauce**

2 tablespoons **olive oil**

1 teaspoon **Chinese 5-spice powder**

400 g/14 oz **chicken breast strips**

250 g/9 oz **new potatoes**, scrubbed, and halved or quartered if large

1 **onion**, chopped

1 **green pepper**, deseeded and cut into chunks

300 g/10½ oz **passata**

2 large **garlic** cloves, crushed

Juice of ½ **lime**

2 handfuls of **kale**, tough stalks removed and leaves finely chopped

Chopped **coriander** leaves (optional), for sprinkling

Crusty wholemeal bread, to serve

What to do

1. Mix together the soy sauce, 1 tablespoon of the oil and the Chinese 5-spice in a large, shallow, non-metallic dish. Add the chicken and turn until it is coated in the marinade. Leave to marinate for at least 30 minutes, longer if you have time.

2. Cook the potatoes in a large saucepan of boiling water for 10 minutes, or until tender, then drain well. Meanwhile, heat a large frying pan over a medium heat. Add the chicken and marinade and cook for 5 minutes, turning, until browned. Scoop out the chicken using a slotted spoon.

3. Add the remaining oil to the pan, if needed, then add the onion and green pepper and cook for 6 minutes until softened. Stir in the passata, garlic, lime juice and 5 tablespoons of water and cook for 5 minutes, stirring occasionally, until the sauce has reduced and thickened. Add the cooked potatoes and chicken to the pan with the kale, stir until mixed together, then cook for another 2–3 minutes until the kale is tender. Serve the chicken sprinkled with the coriander, if using, and with crusty bread on the side.

Try it with tofu

Try replacing the chicken with protein-rich tofu. Drain it, and pat it dry, then marinate it in the spices for about 1 hour. Cook just as for the chicken, for about 5–10 minutes until crisp and golden.

From 7 months

For babies

Soy sauce is a bit too salty for really little ones, so leave it out and then whizz up the pan-fry until it is super-smooth.

Carnival curry + sunshine rice

serves 4 | prep 15 minutes + marinating | cook 20 minutes | freeze me (curry only) | 10+

This creamy Brazilian curry brings carnival to the dinner table. It provides bright colours and tasty, exotic flavours, – all you need to put everyone in the party mood!

What you need

1 **onion**, coarsely grated

2 large **garlic** cloves, coarsely grated

2.5-cm/1-in piece of fresh **root ginger**, peeled and grated

1 teaspoon **mild cayenne pepper**

400 g/14 oz **diced chicken breast**

200 g/7 oz **brown basmati rice**

2 teaspoons **turmeric**

2 tablespoons **coconut or sunflower oil**

1 **red pepper**, deseeded and chopped

200 g/7 oz peeled and deseeded **butternut squash**, cut into bite-sized chunks

200 ml/7 fl oz **coconut milk**

200 ml/7 fl oz reduced-salt **chicken stock**

1 heaped tablespoon **tomato purée**

Juice of 1 **lime**

A handful of chopped **coriander** leaves (optional)

Green vegetables, to serve

What to do

1. Mix half the onion, half the garlic, half the ginger and the cayenne in a shallow dish. Add the chicken and turn to coat. Cover with clingfilm and marinate in the fridge for 1 hour.

2. Put the rice in a saucepan and cover with 400 ml/14 fl oz of water. Bring to the boil, stir in half the turmeric, then reduce the heat to low, cover and simmer for 20 minutes or until the water has been absorbed and the rice is tender. Leave the rice to stand for 5 minutes.

3. Meanwhile, make the curry. Heat the oil in a saucepan and add the remaining onion, garlic and ginger, and the red pepper, cover with a lid and cook for 5 minutes, stirring occasionally, until softened.

4. Add the squash, coconut milk, stock, tomato purée, lime juice and remaining turmeric and cook for 5 minutes, stirring. Add the chicken and the marinade and cook for 5 minutes, or until the chicken is cooked through. Serve sprinkled with coriander, if using, and with the yellow rice and green veggies.

Hot, hot, hot!

If the grown-ups fancy more chilli heat, separate out the little portions, then stir through ½–1 teaspoon more cayenne pepper just before plating up for adults.

Wrapped-up salmon with veggie ribbons

serves 4 | prep 15 minutes | cook 15 minutes | 7+

The whole family is going to love these special foody parcels with the ribbons on the insides! Unwrap the paper and see what delicious treats are in store...

What you need

Olive oil, for brushing and drizzling

4 **salmon fillets**

4 round slices of **lemon**

4 **bay leaves** (optional)

1 **carrot**, peeled and cut into ribbons using a vegetable peeler

1 **courgette**, cut into ribbons using a vegetable peeler

Freshly ground **black pepper**

Green vegetables, to serve

For the crushed potatoes

600 g/1 lb 5 oz **new potatoes**, halved or quartered if large

2 **spring onions**, finely chopped

1–2 tablespoons **olive oil**

2 tablespoons chopped **mint** leaves

What to do

1. Preheat the oven to 180°C/325°F/Gas Mark 4. Place 4 pieces of baking parchment, big enough to wrap the salmon, on a work surface. Brush the parchment with oil, then place a salmon fillet in the centre of each.

2. Squeeze a lemon slice over each salmon fillet, then put the slice on top with a bay leaf, if using. Top with some carrot and courgette. Season with pepper and drizzle over a little oil. Fold the edges of the baking parchment together to make 4 parcels and put them on a baking sheet in the oven for 15 minutes.

3. Meanwhile, cook the potatoes in a saucepan of boiling water for 10–15 minutes until tender. Drain the potatoes, then return them to the pan with the spring onions and oil and crush with the back of a fork or a masher. Stir in the mint and divide among 4 plates.

4. Open the parcels and place the salmon and vegetables on top of the potatoes. You could remove the fish skin first and discard the bay leaves and lemon. Spoon any juices over the top and serve with green vegetables.

88

Family's Meal Planner

foody adventures

	Dinner	This week's special guests	Who needs a lunchbox?

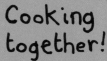

Cooking together!

Let's cook together on

....

Let's make ....

....

....

....

....

....

....

....

The ....
write your name here ➚

This week's

Our family shopping list

1 ....
2 ....
3 ....
4 ....
5 ....
6 ....
7 ....
8 ....
9 ....
10 ....
11 ....
12 ....
13 ....
14 ....
15 ....

	Breakfast	Lunch
Monday		
Tuesday		
Wednesday		
Thursday		
Friday		
Saturday		
Sunday		

...my food is
... rumbling!
...nches and
...dy, suitable
... in bulk
... week!).
...ge so that

Good for baby, too! (10m+)

Spiced brekkie hash-up (p.19)

Zoomy mushrooms (p.24)

Dunkable cheesy broccoli fritters (p.65)

Carnival curry + sunshine rice (p.87)

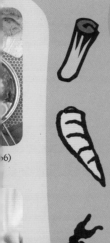

Three-step easy coconut dhal (p.91)

Warm + scrummy meatballs (p.94)

Pop-it-in-the-oven risotto (p.97)

Ultimate beef hotpot with gnocchi (p.101)

Baked mushroom-y pasta (p.105)

Punchy Italian lamb (p.115)

Crispy topped pork stroganoff (p.157)

Dig-in salmon lasagne (p.163)

Slowly-does-it beef pot roast (p.168)

Laid-back crustless quiche (p.171)

Build-it bean burgers (p.68)

Cauliflower pizzette (p.75)

Eastern chicken pan-fry (p.84)

Carnival curry + sunshine rice (p.87)

Three-step easy coconut dhal (p.91)

Warm + scrummy meatballs (p.94)

Dig-in salmon lasagne (p.163)

Slowly-does-it beef pot roast (p.168)

Laid-back crustless quiche (p.171)

Dino ribs in Chinese sauce (p.172)

Stacked-up chicken + quinoa burgers (p.181)

Crisp + crunchy cauliflower tabbouleh (p.182)

...p.65)

What shall we eat today?

Looking at pictures of yu[...]
a great way to get tummi[...]
Use this chart to choose lu[...]
dinners that are super-spe[...]
for babies, or can be cook[...]
(one less meal to cook nex[...]
Stick the chart on your fri[...]
everyone can feel inspired[...]

Fridge to table in under 25 mins

Bubbly green soup (p.49)

Dragon omelette rolls (p.56)

Moon + star flatbread pizza (p.59)

Little monster chickpea stir-fry (p.62)

Eye-spy eggs (p.[...]

Zesty prawn pasta salad (p.71)

Wiggly chicken noodles (p.83)

Sunset jerk chicken (p.106)

Seaside fish + creamy corn dip (p.110)

Punchy Italian lamb (p.115)

Zingy Thai turke[...] noodles (p.116)

Make more to freeze

Hearty red chicken soup (p.45)

Bubbly green soup (p.49)

Fill-you-up tomato + lentil soup (p.52)

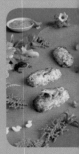
Dunkable chees[...] broccoli fritters

Ultimate beef hotpot with gnocchi (p.101)

Baked mushroom-y pasta (p.105)

Sunset jerk chicken (p.106)

Zingy Thai turkey noodles (p.116)

Goat's cheese ta[...] (p.117)

Three-step easy coconut dhal

serves 4 · prep 10 minutes · cook 30 minutes · freeze me · 10+

Dhal is such a brilliant way to introduce taste explorers to gently spiced lentil curry. This dhal is not only delicious and healthy, but ready in just three easy-peasy steps.

What you need

2 tablespoons **coconut or sunflower oil**

1 **onion**, grated

1 **carrot**, peeled and grated

2 **garlic** cloves, grated

2.5-cm/1-in piece of fresh **root ginger**, peeled and grated

1 tablespoon **garam masala**

1 teaspoon **turmeric**

150 g/5½ oz **split red lentils**

300 ml/10½ fl oz canned **coconut milk**

500 ml/17 fl oz reduced-salt **vegetable stock**

2 good handfuls of **baby spinach leaves**

Apple Raita (optional; see page 177), 4 quartered **hard-boiled eggs**, a sprinkling of **chilli flakes** (optional) and warm **naan bread**, to serve

What to do

1. Heat the oil in a saucepan over a medium heat. Add the onion, carrot, garlic and ginger, cover with a lid and cook for 7 minutes, stirring occasionally, until softened.

2. Stir in the spices, lentils, coconut milk and stock. Bring almost to the boil, then reduce the heat, cover and simmer for 20 minutes. Stir the dhal occasionally to prevent it sticking to the bottom of the pan and add a splash of water if it looks too dry. Stir in the spinach and cook for a couple of minutes until wilted.

3. Serve in bowls topped with the raita, if using, hard-boiled eggs, and a sprinkling of chilli flakes, if using (for the grown ups), with a naan on the side for dunking.

91

Three ways with storecupboard foods

It's the day before your big food shop and you need to be inventive… These suppers, using mostly staples from the food cupboards or the freezer, can help you to create delicious emergency family dinners.

Crispy crumb spaghetti with tuna

serves **4** | prep **5** minutes | cook **15** minutes | freeze me

300 g/10½ oz **spaghetti**
200 g/7 oz **frozen broccoli florets**
2 tablespoons **extra virgin olive oil**
50 g/1¾ oz **wholemeal breadcrumbs**, or made fresh using day-old bread
1 **garlic** clove, finely chopped
Finely grated zest and juice of 1 **lemon**
225 g/8 oz can **tuna chunks** in spring water, drained
1 tablespoon **capers**, patted dry (optional)

Cook the spaghetti in a saucepan of boiling water, following the instructions on the packet (about 10–15 minutes). Meanwhile, steam the broccoli for 2–3 minutes until just tender, then refresh under cold running water.

While the spaghetti and broccoli are cooking, heat 1 tablespoon of oil in a large frying pan. Add the breadcrumbs and fry for 4 minutes, then add the garlic and stir for 1 minute until the crumbs are crisp and light golden. Tip them into a bowl and stir in the lemon zest.

Wipe the frying pan clean, add the remaining oil, then the tuna, broccoli and capers, if using, and heat through. Drain the pasta, reserving the liquid, and add 100 ml/3½ fl oz of the cooking water with the lemon juice to the pan and heat through.

To serve, top the tuna spaghetti with the crumb mixture. (You could turn any leftover pasta and sauce into a tortilla: simply pour beaten eggs over the pasta mixture and cook both sides until set.)

Nutty coconut chicken

serves 4 | prep 15 minutes | cook 10 minutes | freeze me | 10+

- 175 g/6 oz **wholewheat noodles**
- 1 tablespoon **sunflower oil**
- 400 g/14 oz defrosted **frozen chicken breast strips**
- 100 g/3½ oz **frozen sliced mixed peppers**
- 3 **spring onions**, green and white parts separated, sliced
- 85 g/3 oz **frozen peas** or **frozen sliced green beans**
- 2 **garlic** cloves, finely chopped
- 2 teaspoons **garam masala**
- 1 teaspoon **turmeric**
- 2 tablespoons **smooth peanut butter**
- ½ can **coconut milk**

Cook the noodles in a saucepan of boiling water, following the packet instructions, until tender. Drain, refresh under cold running water, then leave to drain.

Meanwhile, heat the oil in a large wok over a high heat. Add the chicken and stir-fry for 4 minutes, or until cooked through. Remove from the wok with a slotted spoon and add the mixed peppers, the white part of the spring onions, the peas or beans and a splash more oil, if needed. Stir-fry for 2 minutes, then add the garlic and spices.

Reduce the heat to medium and add 125 ml/4 fl oz of water, the peanut butter and coconut milk. Stir until combined, then return the chicken to the pan with the noodles and warm through. Serve sprinkled with the green part of the spring onions.

Summer bean + carrot pot

serves 4–6 | prep 10 minutes | cook 30 minutes | freeze me | 10+

- 2 tablespoons **olive oil**
- 1 large **onion**, chopped
- ½ can **chopped tomatoes**
- 375 ml/13 fl oz reduced-salt **vegetable stock**
- 2 teaspoons **dried oregano**
- 1 can **cannellini beans**, drained
- 75 g/2½ oz stale **wholemeal bread**, torn into chunks
- 250 g/9 oz **frozen sliced carrots**
- 175 g/6 oz **frozen peas**
- Wide strips of **lemon** zest and 1 tablespoon lemon juice
- **Bulgar wheat**, to serve

Heat the oil in a flameproof casserole over a medium heat. Add the onion and cook for 5 minutes until softened. Add the tomatoes, stock, oregano and cannellini beans and bring to the boil, then reduce the heat to low, cover with a lid and simmer for 20 minutes, or until the beans are tender. Stir the stew occasionally to prevent it sticking to the bottom of the pan.

Add the bread, carrots, peas and lemon zest and juice to the casserole and cook for 3–5 minutes, stirring occasionally, until the carrots and peas are tender. Remove the zest and serve with bulgar wheat on the side. (It's also delicious topped with a spoonful of hummus, if you have any.)

Warm + scrummy meatballs in gravy

serves **4** (with extra meatballs)
prep **15** minutes
cook **20** minutes
freeze me (meatballs only)
10+

Most families have a tried-and-tested meatball recipe – this is the Ella's Kitchen family favourite. Served with creamy gravy, mashed potatoes and cranberry jelly, these meatballs are warming through and through.

What you need

400 g/14 oz **pork mince**

1 small **onion**, grated

85 g/3 oz **fresh breadcrumbs** (made using day-old bread)

4 tablespoons chopped **dill** (optional)

2 teaspoons **Dijon mustard**

1 **egg**, lightly beaten

2 tablespoons **sunflower oil**

Freshly ground **black pepper**

Mashed potatoes, seasonal vegetables, and **cranberry jelly** (optional), to serve

For the creamy gravy

30 g/1 oz **unsalted butter**

2 tablespoons **plain flour**

500 ml/17 fl oz reduced-salt **beef stock**

2 tablespoons **crème fraîche**

What to do

1. To make the meatballs, mix together the mince, onion, breadcrumbs, half the dill, if using, mustard and egg in a large bowl until combined. Season with pepper. With wet hands, roll the mixture into about 28 meatballs each a little bigger than the size of a large marble.

2. Heat the oil in a large frying pan over a medium–high heat. Add half the meatballs and cook for 5 minutes until browned all over. Remove with a slotted spoon, then cook the remaining meatballs, adding a splash more oil, if needed. Set aside on a plate while you make the sauce.

3. Melt the butter in the same frying pan over a medium–low heat. Stir in the flour and cook for 2 minutes, stirring continuously. Gradually pour in the stock and cook for 5 minutes, stirring continuously, until reduced and thickened. Stir in the crème fraîche, season with pepper, and return the meatballs to the pan. Stir in the remaining dill, if using, and cook until the meatballs have heated through (about 3 minutes). Serve the meatballs and gravy with mashed potatoes and seasonal vegetables, and with a spoonful of cranberry jelly, if using.

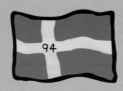

Pop-it-in-the-oven risotto with pesto

serves 4 (with extra pesto)
prep 15 minutes
cook 35 minutes
freeze me 10+ (risotto only)

There are so many reasons to love this brightly coloured risotto. Baking it in the oven means no more standing at the hob stirring away, and the broccoli pesto adds a special topping that crams in the vitamins for the whole family.

What you need

1 tablespoon **olive oil**

15 g/½ oz **unsalted butter**

1 large **onion**, finely chopped

85 g/3 oz **white cabbage**, finely chopped

1 teaspoon **dried oregano**

2 large **garlic** cloves, finely chopped

280 g/10 oz **risotto rice**

400 g/14 oz can **chopped tomatoes**

700 ml/1¼ pints reduced-salt **vegetable stock**

1 tablespoon **tomato purée**

For the broccoli pesto

40 g/1½ oz **cashew nuts**

4 **broccoli** florets (about 70 g/2½ oz)

15 g/½ oz **kale**, tough stalks removed

1 **garlic** clove, peeled

125 ml/4 fl oz **olive oil**

40 g/1½ oz **pecorino or Parmesan cheese**, finely grated, plus extra to serve (optional)

What to do

1. Preheat the oven to 180°C/350°F/Gas Mark 4. Heat the oil and butter in a flameproof casserole over a medium heat. Add the onion and cabbage and cook for 5 minutes, stirring occasionally, until softened.

2. Add the oregano, garlic and rice and cook for about 2 minutes, stirring. Pour in the tomatoes and stock and stir in the tomato purée and bring up to the boil. Stir well until combined, cover with a lid and place in the oven for 25 minutes, stirring halfway, or until the rice is cooked. Remove the risotto from the oven and leave to stand for 5 minutes.

3. Meanwhile, make the broccoli pesto. Put the cashews in a large, dry frying pan and toast over a medium–low heat for 4 minutes, turning once, until golden. Tip into a food processor and blitz until finely chopped. Add the broccoli, kale and garlic and process again until you have a coarse paste (you may have to occasionally scrape the mixture down the sides of the processor so it is evenly mixed).

4. With the motor still running, gradually pour in the oil until blended. Finally, stir in the pecorino or Parmesan. Serve the risotto topped with a good spoonful of the pesto and grate over extra cheese, if you like.

Munchy cheese + leek sausages

These meat-free sausages are crunchy on the outside and cheesy in the middle. Serve them up with our own Special Baked Beans (see page 51) on the side. (If you're serving with baked potatoes, don't forget to put them in the oven before you start on the sausages.)

What you need

20 g/¾ oz **unsalted butter**

200 g/7 oz **leeks**, finely chopped

200 g/7 oz fresh **breadcrumbs** (made using day-old bread)

2 teaspoons **dried thyme**

2 teaspoons **English mustard**

2 **eggs**, separated

140 g/5 oz **Cheddar cheese**, grated

Sunflower oil, for frying

Special Baked Beans (see page 51), baked **potato** and **vegetables**, to serve

What to do

1. Heat the butter in a large frying pan over a medium heat. Add the leeks and cook for 5 minutes, stirring often, until softened.

2. Meanwhile, put 150 g/5½ oz of the breadcrumbs in a large bowl with the thyme. Beat the mustard and egg yolks together and add to the bowl. Add the cooked leeks and the cheese and stir until combined. With damp hands, shape the mixture into 8 sausages. Chill for 30 minutes, if time allows.

3. Heat the oven to 180°C/350°F/Gas Mark 4. Lightly whisk the egg whites in a shallow bowl and put the remaining breadcrumbs in a separate shallow bowl.

4. Heat enough oil to cover the base of a large frying pan over a medium heat. Dunk each sausage into the egg white and then coat in breadcrumbs and place in the pan. Cook the sausages for 5 minutes, turning, until golden all over, then place them on a baking sheet and bake in the oven for 10 minutes until cooked through. Drain on kitchen paper and serve with Special Baked Beans, baked potato, and veg on the side.

Can I help?

Shape up!

Show your little helper how to roll the mixture and shape the sausages so that they're just right!

Ultimate beef hotpot with gnocchi dumplings

serves 4–6 | prep 15 minutes | cook 1½ hours | freeze me | 10+

Wonderfully comforting, feel-good food, a hotpot is the perfect lure to the family table. This version is especially satisfying thanks to the nutritious green lentils that provide iron, protein and fibre, and has an easy-to-make topping of squidgy, cheesy gnocchi. Mmmm...

What you need

2 tablespoons **olive oil**

2 **leeks**, trimmed and sliced

2 **carrots**, peeled and diced

2 **parsnips**, peeled and diced

400 g/14 oz **braising steak**, cut into bite-sized pieces

450 ml/16 fl oz reduced-salt **beef stock**

1 tablespoon **tomato purée**

1 long **rosemary** sprig

1 **bay leaf**

100 g/3½ oz drained canned **green lentils**

500 g/1 lb 2 oz ready-made **gnocchi**

30 g/1 oz **mature Cheddar cheese**, grated

Green vegetables, to serve

Get ahead!

You can make the hotpot filling two days in advance of serving. When you're ready to cook, heat the filling through on the hob, top it with the gnocchi and cheese and grill to finish.

What to do

1) Preheat the oven to 180°C/350°F/Gas Mark 4. Heat half the oil in a large flameproof casserole dish over a medium heat. Add the leeks, carrots and parsnips and cook for 5 minutes until softened.

2) Using a slotted spoon, remove the vegetables and set aside. Add the remaining oil and brown the beef all over for 5 minutes. Return the vegetables to the casserole with the stock, tomato purée, rosemary and bay leaf and bring to the boil. Stir, cover with a lid and put the casserole in the oven for 45 minutes.

3) Meanwhile, blend the lentils to a coarse paste or mash with a potato masher. Remove the rosemary from the casserole and stir in the lentils. Cover with a lid and cook in the oven for another 30 minutes, adding more stock or water if needed, or until the beef is tender.

4) Meanwhile, cook the gnocchi in a large saucepan of boiling water, following the packet instructions, then drain well.

5) Preheat the grill to medium–high. Spoon the gnocchi on top of the casserole, scatter the cheese over the top and place the casserole under the grill for 10 minutes, or until the cheese has melted. Leave to cool slightly, then serve with green vegetables.

101

Time for table talk

Family life can be so busy, but mealtimes are a good chance for everyone to get talking together. This activity creates a chit-chat lucky dip to bring out when you're round the table. You'll need a large jar or plastic tub with a lid, as well as paper and pens.

1

Make a topic jar

Give everyone 5 slips of paper each. Write down or draw: on the first slip, an animal; on the next, a type of food; then a feeling, a place, and something random. Give little ones help if they need it. Fold each slip of paper in half and pop all the slips of paper in the jar. (Don't worry if there are duplicate ideas; it's all part of the fun.)

② Add some questions

Give everyone another slip of paper. This time, pop a question on it – the sillier the better! Don't forget that 'open' (rather than 'yes or no') questions work best. The box, right, has some ideas to get you started. Help anyone who needs it, then fold the bits of paper, pop them in the topic jar and seal with the lid ready for your next family mealtime.

What can I ask?

To get you started, here are some ideas for questions you could put in your jar. Don't forget to add your own and always ask why you each choose the answers you do.

☺ If you could eat only one food for a year what would it be?

☺ If you could have a super power what would it be?

☺ If you had 3 wishes what would they be?

☺ Where would you fly if you had wings?

☺ If you could be invisible for a day, what would you do?

☺ If you had a pet dragon what would you call it and what would you do together?

☺ If you were a cartoon character which one would you be?

☺ What adventure do you wish you could go on right now?

☺ If you could invite one person – a friend, a famous person, a character from a book or film – to tea, who would you have?

③ Talk about it!

At the start of a family meal, take it in turns to put your hand in the jar and pull out a slip of paper. Then, read the topic or question aloud and get chatting! If it's a word, what does it make each of you think of? How does it smell? What does it look like, and so on? If it's a question, give everyone a turn to answer.

④ We've finished!

When you've been through all the slips of paper in the jar, start again with new topics and questions. Feel free to think of your own subjects – be as inventive as you can be!

Baked mushroom-y pasta

serves 4 | prep 10 minutes | cook 35 minutes | freeze me 10+ (cooked or uncooked)

Pasta bake makes a fantastic mid-week dinner. This one takes just 10 minutes to prepare, then everything else happens all by itself in the oven. It's easy *and* delicious – perfect!

What you need

1 tablespoon **olive oil**, plus extra for drizzling

1 large **onion**, chopped

1 **carrot**, peeled and grated

300 g/10½ oz **mushrooms**, chopped

3 **garlic** cloves, chopped

400 g/14 oz can **chopped tomatoes**

200 ml/7 fl oz **vegetable or porcini stock**

3 tablespoons **basil pesto**

280 g/10 oz **penne pasta**

125 g/4½ oz **mozzarella cheese**, drained, and torn into pieces

30 g/1 oz **chopped walnuts**

What to do

1) Heat the oil in a large frying pan over a medium heat. Add the onion and carrot and cook for 5 minutes, stirring occasionally, until softened. Stir in the mushrooms and cook for 5 minutes, or until tender and there is no trace of liquid in the pan. Add the garlic and then the tomatoes, stock and pesto. Bring to the boil, then reduce the heat to low, cover with a lid and simmer for 5 minutes until reduced and thickened.

2) Meanwhile, preheat the oven to 200°C/400°F/ Gas Mark 6. Cook the pasta in a saucepan of boiling water, following the instructions on the pack, until just cooked (about 8–10 minutes), then drain and return it to the pan. Pour the sauce over the pasta and turn until combined.

3) Transfer the pasta and sauce to an ovenproof dish, scatter over the mozzarella and walnuts and drizzle over a little extra oil, then bake for 20 minutes, or until the cheese has melted.

Speedy no-bake!

If you're short of time, you can cook the sauce for 10 minutes longer, then just stir it through the pasta and serve without baking. You won't get the golden oozy cheesiness on top, but you'll have everyone filled up sooner.

Sunset jerk chicken with ginger mash

serves 4 · prep 10 minutes · cook 15 minutes · freeze me
+ marinating

Packed with all the flavours of the Caribbean, this jerk-style chicken will have you all bopping to reggae beats by bedtime.

What you need

4 skinless, boneless **chicken breasts** (about 450 g/1 lb)

2 teaspoons **ground allspice**

2 teaspoons **paprika**

1 tablespoon **clear honey**

2 tablespoons **olive oil**

1 **red chilli**, deseeded and diced (optional)

Green vegetables, to serve

For the ginger squash mash

1 **butternut squash**, peeled, deseeded and cut into chunks

2 large **garlic** cloves, peeled and left whole

5-cm/2-in piece of fresh **root ginger**, peeled and sliced into thin rounds

1 tablespoon **unsalted butter**

What to do

1. Put the chicken breasts between 2 sheets of clingfilm and bash with the end of a rolling pin or meat mallet to an even thickness about 1 cm/½ in thick.

2. Mix together the allspice, paprika, honey and olive oil in a large, shallow dish. Add the flattened chicken breasts and turn until they are coated in the marinade. Leave to marinate for 30 minutes or longer, if you have time, or cook straightaway.

3. To make the mash, put the squash, garlic and ginger in a saucepan and cover with water. Bring to a gentle boil over a medium heat, then reduce the heat and cook for 10–15 minutes, part-covered with a lid, until tender.

4. To cook the chicken, heat a large griddle pan over a high heat. Add the chicken, reduce the heat to medium and cook the chicken for 5–6 minutes, turning once, until cooked through and no longer pink (you may have to cook it in two batches). Keep warm.

5. When the squash is cooked, drain it and return it to the pan with the garlic, discarding the ginger. Add the butter and mash until fairly smooth, then spoon it onto serving plates. Slice the chicken and place on top of the mash, sprinkle with chilli, if using, and serve with steamed green vegetables.

Squashy soup

Ginger squash mash makes a great base for an easy soup. Add onions, carrots and celery to the squash, stir in some low-salt vegetable stock, simmer until the veggies are tender, then purée until smooth.

106

Take-away prawn balls + mango sauce

serves 4 | prep 20 minutes | cook 10 minutes | freeze me

+ chilling

These bite-sized fish balls are perfect for nibbling on when you're watching a movie with your favourite people – it's tasty take-away-style food made at home!

What you need

225 g/8 oz fresh raw **tiger prawns**, patted dry

300 g/10½ oz fresh skinless, boneless, **white fish fillets**, patted dry and cut into chunks

1 **shallot**, cut into wedges

1 **garlic** clove, peeled and left whole

½ teaspoon **English mustard**

1 teaspoon **thyme**

½ teaspoon **mild cayenne pepper**

2 teaspoons **sweet paprika**

Juice of 1 **lime**

A little **flour**, for dusting

Sunflower oil, for frying

Brown rice (cooked with 1 teaspoon **turmeric**) and **salad**, to serve

For the fruity sauce

250 g/9 oz peeled, stoned **mango**, cut into chunks

Juice of 1 **lime**

¼ teaspoon **dried chilli flakes** (optional)

What to do

1. To make the fish balls, put the prawns, white fish, shallot, garlic, mustard, thyme, spices and lime juice in a food processor and blitz to a coarse paste.

2. Generously coat a plate and your hands with flour. Form the fish mixture into 16 walnut-sized balls, then roll them in the flour to coat lightly. The fish mixture is quite loose but holds together when shaped into a ball. Put the balls on a plate, flatten the tops slightly and chill in the fridge for 30 minutes to firm up.

3. Meanwhile, make the fruity sauce. Blend together the chunks of mango with the lime juice and pour the mixture into a bowl. You can add a few chilli flakes, if you like.

4. To cook the balls, generously coat a large frying pan with oil and heat over a medium heat. Add half the balls, or enough so the pan is not too full, and fry for 4 minutes, turning frequently, until golden all over. Keep the first batch warm in a low oven on kitchen paper while you cook the second lot. Serve the balls with the fruity sauce, rice and salad.

Seaside fish + creamy corn dip

All the family will love these flavoursome fingers of fish. The polenta gives them a satisfying crispy crunch and the buttery creamed corn is perfect for dipping.

What you need

4 **white fish fillets**, such as cod, hake, haddock or pollock, cut into chunky fingers

1 **egg**

55 g/2 oz **instant polenta**

25 g/1 oz **Parmesan cheese**, finely grated

½ teaspoon **dried oregano** (optional)

2 tablespoons **sunflower oil**

New potatoes and **green vegetables**, to serve

For the creamy corn

25 g/1 oz **unsalted butter**

425 g/15 oz no-sugar, no-salt canned **sweetcorn**, drained

1–2 tablespoons **crème fraîche**

5 tablespoons **whole milk**

What to do

1. To make the creamy corn, melt the butter in a saucepan over a medium–low heat. Add the corn and cook for 4 minutes, stirring occasionally, until tender. Stir in the crème fraîche and milk, warm through, then use a hand blender to blend until creamy, adding more crème fraîche or milk if needed.

2. Meanwhile, pat the fish dry with kitchen paper. Beat the egg in a shallow bowl. Mix together the polenta, Parmesan and oregano, if using, in a separate shallow bowl.

3. Heat the oil in a large frying pan over a medium heat. Dip the fish fingers into the egg and then into the polenta mixture until coated. Place the fish fingers straight into the pan. Cook the fish fingers for 2–3 minutes on each side, or until cooked through and crisp.

4. Reheat the creamy corn and serve with the crispy fish fingers, new potatoes and extra vegetables. Or serve the fish in cones, as if you were at the seaside!

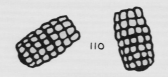

Three ways with a tomato-y sauce

Here is one tasty basic tomato sauce that you can use three ways! Make a big batch of the sauce, freeze it in portions, then reinvent it. Easy!

Basic tomato sauce

serves 3-4 | prep 10 minutes | cook 20 minutes | freeze me 7+

1 tablespoon **olive oil**

1 **onion**, finely chopped

1 **carrot**, peeled and grated

1 **celery** stick, finely chopped

2 **garlic** cloves, chopped

400 g/14 oz can **chopped tomatoes**

1 tablespoon **tomato purée**

100 ml/3½ fl oz reduced-salt **vegetable stock**

Heat the oil in a saucepan over a medium heat. Add the onion, carrot and celery, cover with a lid and cook for 8 minutes, stirring occasionally, until softened. Stir in the garlic and cook for 1 minute.

Add the tomatoes, tomato purée and stock and bring to the boil, then reduce the heat to low, part-cover with a lid and simmer for 5–10 minutes until reduced and thickened. Cook the sauce for the shorter time if you are using it in one of the mince dishes that follow, or cook for the longer time if serving the sauce on its own.

Mexi-mole

serves 6-8 | prep 10 minutes | cook 25 minutes | freeze me

125 g/4½ oz **butternut squash**

2 tablespoons **olive oil**

250 g/9 oz **lean beef mince**

1 quantity **Basic Tomato Sauce**

200 g/7 oz can **red kidney beans**, drained

2 heaped teaspoons **Cajun spice**

1 teaspoon **dried thyme**

Juice of 1 **lime**

½ teaspoon **cocoa powder**

1 chopped **avocado** and **brown basmati rice**, to serve

Preheat the oven to 200°C/400°F/Gas Mark 6. Peel and cube the squash and toss it in half the oil to coat. Tip onto a baking tray and roast for 25 minutes, until tender.

Meanwhile, heat the remaining oil in a pan over a medium heat. Add the mince and cook for 5 minutes until browned. Add the tomato sauce, beans, Cajun spice and thyme and bring to the boil. Cover and simmer over a low heat for 20 minutes until the sauce has thickened. Stir in the cooked squash, half the lime juice and the cocoa powder. Toss the avocado in the remaining lime juice. Serve the mole with rice and topped with avocado.

Chinese ginger pork

serves 6–8 • prep 5 minutes • cook 25 minutes • freeze me

2 teaspoons **sunflower oil**

250 g/9 oz **lean pork mince**

150 g/5½ oz **mushrooms**, chopped

2.5-cm/1-in piece of fresh **root ginger**, grated (no need to peel)

1 quantity **Basic Tomato Sauce**

1 teaspoon **sesame oil**

2 teaspoons **Chinese 5-spice powder**

4 teaspoons reduced-salt **soy sauce**

Juice of 1 **lime**

4 large handfuls of **spinach**, tough stalks removed

200 g/7 oz **wholemeal noodles**

2 **spring onions**, finely chopped (optional)

Heat the oil in a large wok over a high heat. Add the pork mince and then the mushrooms and stir-fry for 5 minutes, or until the pork has browned and the mushrooms softened. Add a splash more oil, if needed.

Reduce the heat to medium–low, stir in the ginger followed by the tomato sauce, sesame oil, five-spice and soy sauce and cook for 15 minutes, stirring frequently, until reduced and thickened. Add the lime juice and spinach and cook until the spinach has wilted, adding a splash of water if the sauce is dry.

Cook the noodles in a saucepan of boiling water, until tender. Drain. Sprinkle the ginger pork with the spring onions, if using, and serve with the noodles. Leftover pork will keep in the fridge for up to 3 days.

Moussaka-style pasta

serves 6–8 • prep 5 minutes • cook 30 minutes • freeze me 7+

1 tablespoon **olive oil**

250 g/9 oz **lean lamb mince**

1 **aubergine**, cut into small cubes

1 quantity **Basic Tomato Sauce**

1–2 teaspoons **dried thyme**, to taste

2 teaspoons **ground cumin**

1 small **cinnamon stick**

300 g/10½ oz **penne pasta**

Feta cheese, crumbled, for sprinkling

Freshly ground **black pepper**

Heat the oil in a large saucepan over a medium–high heat. Add the lamb mince and then the aubergine and cook for 8 minutes, stirring, or until the lamb has browned and the aubergine softened.

Stir in the tomato sauce, thyme, cumin and cinnamon and bring to the boil, then reduce the heat to medium–low, cover with a lid and simmer for 20 minutes, stirring occasionally, until the mince is tender. Remove the cinnamon stick and season with a little pepper.

Meanwhile, cook the pasta in a saucepan of boiling water, following the instructions on the packet. Drain, adding a splash of the pasta cooking water to the sauce if it looks dry. Serve the pasta topped with the sauce with a sprinkling of feta cheese.

Turin

Milan

Venice

Rome

Bari

Naples

Punchy Italian lamb

serves **4** | prep **10** minutes | cook **15** minutes | freeze me

+ marinating | *(plain sauce or sauce with lamb chopped in only)*

Southern Italian puttanesca sauce is the inspiration for this super-tasty lamb dish. You could make double the sauce quantity and then freeze the extra to use stirred through spaghetti another time. *Bellissima!*

What you need

2 tablespoons **olive oil**

Juice of 1 **lemon**

2 **rosemary** sprigs, leaves of one finely chopped

3–4 **lamb steaks or loin chops**, depending on size

1 tablespoon **small capers**, drained and patted dry (optional)

3 **garlic** cloves, chopped

2 **anchovy fillets** in oil, drained and finely chopped (optional)

400 g/14 oz can **chopped tomatoes**

A handful of **pitted black olives**, chopped

A handful of **raisins**

1 teaspoon **dried oregano**

Dried chilli flakes, for sprinkling (optional)

Freshly ground **black pepper**

Mashed potatoes and **green vegetables**, to serve

What to do

1. Put half the oil, the lemon juice and chopped rosemary in a non-metallic dish and season with pepper. Add the lamb and turn until coated in the oil mixture. Cover the dish and leave to marinate for 30 minutes, if time allows.

2. If serving the capers, heat the remaining olive oil in a large sauté pan. Add the capers and fry over a medium heat for 1–2 minutes until crisp (take care as they can spit). Scoop out the capers, leaving the oil in the pan, and drain on kitchen paper. (If not using capers, heat the oil in the pan and follow step 3.)

3. Turn the heat to medium–low, add the garlic, anchovies, if using, tomatoes, olives, raisins, rosemary sprig and oregano to the pan, part-cover with a lid and cook for 10 minutes, stirring occasionally, until reduced and thickened. (The anchovies will melt into the sauce.) Remove the rosemary.

4. Meanwhile, heat a griddle pan or frying pan over a medium–high heat. Add the lamb and cook for 5 minutes, turning once, or until cooked to your liking. Leave the lamb to rest, covered, on a warm plate for 5 minutes.

5. Serve the lamb with the sauce, sprinkled with crispy capers (adults may like to add a sprinkling of chilli flakes) with mash and green veg on the side.

For babies

From 10 months

Leave out the capers and anchovy fillets as they'll be a bit too salty for little ones. Mash or chop to your baby's usual texture.

Zingy Thai turkey noodles

There's lots of citrus flavour in this Thai-inspired noodle dish. Made with turkey (which is naturally super-lean) and packed with four different veggies, it's healthy for everyone.

What you need

2 tablespoons **sunflower oil**

350 g/12 oz **turkey mince**

6 large **spring onions**, chopped

1 **orange pepper**, deseeded and chopped

150 g/5½ oz **white cabbage**, finely shredded

2 large **garlic** cloves, finely chopped

2.5-cm/1-in piece of fresh **root ginger**, grated

1 stick **lemongrass**, tough outer leaves removed and inside finely chopped

2 **kaffir lime leaves** (optional)

1 tablespoon reduced-salt **soy sauce**

1 **courgette**, grated

175 g/6 oz **wholemeal noodles**

300 ml/10 fl oz reduced-salt **chicken stock**

A handful chopped **coriander** leaves (optional)

What to do

1. Heat half the oil in a large wok and stir-fry the turkey for 5 minutes, or until cooked through. Remove with a slotted spoon and leave to one side.

2. Pour off any liquid in the wok and add the remaining oil. Reserve some of the green parts of the spring onions and add the rest to the wok with the orange pepper and cabbage and fry for 3 minutes. Add the garlic, ginger, lemongrass, kaffir lime leaves, if using, soy sauce and courgette and fry for 1 minute.

3. Meanwhile, cook the noodles, following the packet instructions (about 5 minutes), until tender. Drain and put into serving bowls.

4. Return the turkey to the wok, add the stock and warm through, then spoon on top of the noodles. Sprinkle with the reserved spring onions and the coriander, if using, then serve at once.

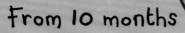

From 10 months

For babies

Soy sauce is a bit too salty for little ones, so leave it out. Then, chop up the dish to your baby's usual texture.

Goat's cheese tart with ruby-red dip

A perfect in-between snack for grown-ups, this goat's cheese tart, sliced into fingers, is also a fun kids' tea. Share it with a buddy who's come to play.

What you need

Olive oil, for brushing and greasing

320 g/11½ oz chilled **ready-rolled puff pastry** sheet

A little **flour**, for dusting

2 **eggs**

2½ tablespoons **whole milk**

1 teaspoon **thyme** leaves

60 g/2¼ oz soft, crumbly **goat's cheese**

85 g/3 oz **sun-dried tomatoes in oil**, very finely chopped

Freshly ground **black pepper**

For the ruby-red dip

1 large **red pepper**, deseeded and quartered

2 **tomatoes**

1 teaspoon **clear honey**

1 teaspoon **apple cider vinegar**

What to do

1. Preheat the oven to 220°C/425°F/Gas Mark 7. To make the dip, brush the red pepper and tomatoes with olive oil, and roast for 15–20 minutes, until the pepper is soft and coloured.

2. Meanwhile, roll out the pastry slightly on a flour-dusted work surface and place it on a greased baking sheet. Fold the edges by 1 cm/½ in, making a raised border.

3. Beat the eggs and use a little to brush the edges of the tart. Stir the milk into the remaining egg with the thyme and goat's cheese and beat until smooth. Spoon the sun-dried tomatoes evenly over the pastry, then top with the egg mixture. Bake for 20–25 minutes until risen and golden.

4. While the tart is baking, blitz together the dip ingredients until coarse. Cut the tart into slices or fingers and serve with a bowl of the dip.

Let's make tea!

Can I help?

This tart is so simple, it makes a fun playdate activity as well as a perfect tea. Ask your helpers to fold the pastry edges, beat the eggy mixture and spoon on the tomatoes. Then they can go and play until it's ready for eating!

Tasty treats and puds

Bite-sized banoffee tartlets

makes **12** | prep **15** minutes | cook **20** minutes | freeze me (pastry cases only)
+ chilling
+ soaking

Creamy, yogurty mixture spooned into cases of special nutty pastry and topped with a slice of banana and chocolate sprinkles – these are little treats to bring on the biggest smiles!

What you need

175 g/6 oz ready-to-eat **dried dates**

1 teaspoon **vanilla extract**

4 tablespoons **thick double cream**

3 tablespoons **thick natural yogurt**

1 **banana**, sliced

Cocoa powder, for dusting

For the almond pastry

125 g/4½ oz **plain flour**, plus extra for dusting

40 g/1½ oz **ground almonds**

85 g/3 oz chilled **unsalted butter**, diced

1 **egg yolk**

What to do

1. First make the pastry. Mix together the flour and almonds in a large bowl. Rub in the butter, using your fingertips, until the mixture resembles fine breadcrumbs. Mix in the egg yolk and 1 tablespoon cold water using a fork and then your hands to a make a ball of dough. Wrap the pastry in clingfilm and chill in the fridge for 30 minutes.

2. While the pastry is chilling, put the dates in a bowl, cover with boiling water and leave to soften for 20 minutes. Drain, reserving 3 tablespoons of the soaking water. Blend the dates, reserved water and half the vanilla until smooth. Leave to one side.

3. Preheat the oven to 200°C/400°F/Gas Mark 6. Lightly grease a 12-hole patty tin.

4. Roll out the pastry on a lightly floured work surface until about 3 mm/⅛ in thick. Use a fluted pastry cutter to cut out 12 x 9-cm/3½-in rounds of dough, re-rolling the pastry when needed. Lightly press the rounds into the holes of the prepared tin. Bake for 20 minutes, or until cooked and light golden. Turn out on to a wire rack and leave to cool.

5. Divide the date mixture between the pastry cases, smoothing the tops. Mix together the cream, yogurt and remaining vanilla, and spoon it on top of the date mixture. Top with a slice of banana and dust with a little cocoa.

Special choc pots

What makes these silky pots of chocolate so special? They're made using avocado! Chocolate dessert with a wholesome green twist? Now everyone's happy!

What you need

70 g/2½ oz ready-to-eat **dried dates**

1 teaspoon **coconut oil**

55 g/2 oz **blanched hazelnuts**

1 small ripe **avocado**, halved, stoned and flesh scooped out

4 teaspoons **unsweetened cocoa powder**

1 teaspoon **vanilla extract**

2–3 teaspoons **maple syrup** or **clear honey**, to taste

100 ml/3½ fl oz **whole milk**

6 tablespoons **whipping cream** or **Greek yogurt**, and **strawberries** or **raspberries**, to serve

Brrr... freeze it!

Don't throw away leftover avocado. Instead, peel the avocado and remove the pit, then mash the flesh with 1 tablespoon of lemon juice. Spoon it into an airtight bag, squeeze out all the air and seal. Freeze for up to 1 year.

What to do

1. Put the dates in a heatproof bowl and pour over 6 tablespoons just-boiled water. Stir in the coconut oil until melted, then leave to soak for 30 minutes until softened.

2. Meanwhile, put the hazelnuts in a large, dry frying pan and toast them over a medium–low heat for 5 minutes, turning often, until starting to colour. Tip the nuts into a bowl and leave to cool.

3. Set aside 5 hazelnuts, then put the rest of the nuts in a food processor and process until very finely chopped. Add the avocado, cocoa powder, vanilla, maple syrup or honey and milk to the processor. Drain the dates, reserving the soaking water, and add them to the processor with 3 tablespoons of the water. Process until the mixture is smooth and creamy, adding more water if needed.

4. Spoon the chocolate mousse into 4 ramekins and chill for at least 15 minutes to firm up.

5. Meanwhile, finely chop the reserved hazelnuts, whip the cream, if using, and prepare the berries. To serve, spoon the yogurt or whipped cream on top of the pots, followed by the berries, then sprinkle the finely chopped nuts over the top.

Hummingbird cake

This light and fluffy banana and pineapple sponge cake is inspired by a recipe all the way from Jamaica. It's got a tropical zing that will make you hum with joy after every bite!

What you need

150 g/5½ oz **unsalted butter**, melted and cooled, plus extra for greasing

125 g/4½ oz **self-raising flour**, plus extra for dusting

100 g/3½ oz **self-raising wholemeal flour**

2 teaspoons **mixed spice**

1 heaped teaspoon **baking powder**

40 g/1½ oz **unsweetened desiccated coconut**

3 large **eggs**, lightly beaten

1 teaspoon **vanilla extract**

150 g/5½ oz **unrefined caster sugar**

3 **bananas**, mashed

225 g/8 oz cored **pineapple**, cut into bite-sized chunks

50 g/1¾ oz **walnut pieces**

For the vanilla cream frosting

280 g/10 oz **cream cheese**

50 g/1¾ oz **unsalted butter**

3 tablespoons **clear honey**

2 teaspoons **vanilla extract**

What to do

1. Preheat the oven to 180°C/350°F/Gas Mark 4. Grease and flour the sides and line the bases of two 20-cm/8-in springform cake tins.

2. Sift together both types of flour, the mixed spice and baking powder into a large bowl, adding any bran left in the sieve. Mix in the coconut, then make a well in the centre.

3. Whisk together the butter, eggs, vanilla and sugar for about 3 minutes until light and fluffy. Stir in the bananas and half the pineapple, then fold the wet ingredients into the dry ingredients. Spoon the mixture into the prepared cake tins. Bake for 35–40 minutes until risen and a skewer inserted in the centre comes out clean.

4. Meanwhile, to make the cream frosting, beat together all the ingredients until smooth and creamy. Leave to chill in the fridge to firm up.

5. Remove the cakes from the oven and leave to cool in the tins for 5 minutes, then turn out onto a wire rack to cool completely.

6. Spread half the frosting over one cake, top it with the second cake and spread the remaining frosting over the top. Decorate with the remaining pineapple and the walnuts.

124

Just-for-one mini cheesecakes

These cheesecakes may be little in size, but they're big on the flavour of tangy lemon and fragrant peaches. Made in a muffin tin, each cheesecake is a perfect size just for one.

What you need

For the base

40 g/1½ oz **unsalted butter**, plus extra for greasing

80 g/3 oz **pecan nuts**

50 g/1¾ oz **porridge oats**

30 g/1 oz **ground almonds**

1 tablespoon **maple syrup** or **clear honey**

For the filling

175 g/6 oz **cream cheese**

100 g/3½ oz **natural yogurt**

Finely grated rind of 1 **lemon** and juice of ½ lemon

2 tablespoons **maple syrup** or **clear honey**

1 teaspoon **vanilla extract**

1 large **egg**, lightly beaten

1½ teaspoons **cornflour**

4 ripe **peaches**, halved, stoned and chopped

What to do

1. Preheat the oven to 180°C/350°F/Gas Mark 4. Grease and line 10 holes of a muffin tin with baking parchment by cutting 2 folded strips of baking parchment and pressing them into the first hole to form a cross shape. Repeat with the remaining holes.

2. To make the cheesecake base, whiz the pecans and oats in a mini food processor, then tip them into a bowl and stir in the ground almonds. Melt the butter in a small saucepan with the maple syrup or honey, then stir it into the pecan mixture. Divide the mixture evenly among the prepared muffin tin holes and press it down to make a firm base. Bake for 5 minutes, then remove from the oven.

3. To make the filling, beat together all the ingredients, apart from the peaches, until smooth and creamy. Spoon the mixture over the nutty base and level the tops, then return to the oven for a further 15–20 minutes until firm and just set – the filling should still have a slight wobble. Leave to cool in the tin, then chill for 20 minutes.

4. When ready to serve, remove the cheesecakes from the muffin tin and peel off the paper strips. Spoon the peaches on top before serving.

For babies

From 10 months

Make the cheesecakes with maple syrup instead of honey to serve to babies. A mashed-up half portion will be enough.

Easy-peasy fruity crumbles

makes 4 · prep 10 minutes · cook 10 minutes · freeze me (fruit only)

Little hands will love to help layer up the fruit and crunchy crumble mix in these no-bake individual crumbles. They are so easy to put together, they're sure to become an instant family favourite.

What you need

1 large ripe **pear**, quartered, cored and chopped

5 **purple plums**, halved, stoned and chopped

100 g/3½ oz **blackberries** or **blueberries**

Finely grated rind and juice of 1 **orange**

4 **cloves**

½ **cinnamon stick**

250 ml/8 fl oz **thick natural yogurt**

For the crumble mix

5 tablespoons **jumbo porridge oats**

2 tablespoons **sunflower seeds**

25 g/1 oz **walnuts**

25 g/1 oz **pecan nuts**

½ teaspoon **ground cinnamon**

2 teaspoons **clear honey**, plus extra to taste

Morning after

You could turn the crumble mixture into a yummy breakfast granola by stirring in some chopped dried fruit.

What to do

1. Put the pear, plums, blackberries or blueberries, orange rind and juice, cloves and cinnamon in a saucepan and bring almost to the boil, then reduce the heat, part-cover with a lid and simmer for 10 minutes, or until reduced and thickened. Leave to cool, remove the cloves and cinnamon stick, and mash the fruit with the back of a fork.

2. Meanwhile, make the crumble topping. Put the oats in a large, dry frying pan and toast for 4 minutes over a medium–low heat, tossing the pan frequently, until they start to turn golden. Tip the oats into a mini food processor. Add the seeds to the pan and toast for 2 minutes or until starting to colour. Tip the seeds into the food processor with the oats.

3. Put the nuts in the pan and toast for another 4 minutes, turning once, or until starting to colour. Add them to the food processor with the oats and seeds and blitz briefly to a coarse crumble. Transfer to a bowl and stir in the cinnamon and honey until everything is coated. Leave to cool.

4. To serve, place 2 tablespoons of the crumble mixture in the bottom of a glass or tumbler and top with a layer of yogurt, then fruit, more crumble and yogurt and a final layer of the crumble mixture. Repeat until you have made 4 crumbles. For small children, serve a smaller portion in a suitable bowl.

128

Sticky sesame bananas

serves **4** · prep **5** minutes · cook **10** minutes

Take a banana, make it sticky, then sprinkle over some seeds – it's food that's fun to help with and delicious to eat. Who can stretch highest as they sprinkle?

What you need

2 teaspoons **sesame seeds**

30 g/1 oz **coconut oil** or **unsalted butter**

4 small **bananas**, peeled and halved lengthways

1 tablespoon **maple syrup** or **clear honey**

4 tablespoons **coconut drinking milk**

Thick natural yogurt, to serve

What to do

1. Put the sesame seeds in a large, dry frying pan over a medium–low heat and toast for 3 minutes, stirring occasionally, or until they start to turn golden. Tip into a bowl and leave to one side.

2. Melt the coconut oil or butter in the frying pan over a medium heat. Add the bananas and cook for 3 minutes until golden, turning once, and spooning the oil over the bananas as they cook.

3. Place the bananas on serving plates. Add the maple syrup or honey and the coconut drinking milk to the pan, stir and cook briefly over a low heat until caramelized. Spoon the sauce over the bananas, sprinkle with sesame seeds and serve with yogurt.

Strawberry clouds

serves 4 | prep 15 minutes | cook 10 minutes

Oh-so floaty, these light, sweet omelettes are like delicious clouds on your plate.
Just be careful they don't float away before you eat them all up!

What you need

300 g/10 oz **strawberries**, hulled and halved

3 **eggs**, separated and set aside individually

2 teaspoons **clear honey**

1 teaspoon **vanilla extract**

2 teaspoons **coconut or sunflower oil**

Thick cream or **natural yogurt** and 2 handfuls of **blueberries**, halved, to serve

What to do

1. Mash or purée half the strawberries to make a fruit sauce, then set aside. Using a hand whisk, whisk the egg whites in a grease-free bowl until they form soft peaks. Gradually add the honey and vanilla, whisking until the whites are stiff and glossy. Fold in the yolks.

2. Preheat the grill to medium–high. Melt half the oil in a large frying pan with a heatproof handle and swirl to coat the base. Tip a large serving spoonful of the frothy egg mixture into the pan and spread it out with a spatula into a round. Repeat with a second serving spoonful to cook two 'clouds' at once. Cook over a medium–low heat for 2–3 minutes until the base is set and light golden. Transfer the pan to the grill and cook the top until just set.

3. Slide the 'clouds' onto a serving plate and top with mashed or puréed strawberries, the cream or yogurt and the halved strawberries and blueberries. Repeat, making clouds two at a time, until all the mixture is used up.

Ella's shortcut

Instead of making a strawberry sauce, use 1 x 120 g pouch of Ella's Kitchen strawberries + apples.

Four ways with fruit

Encouraging little ones to eat a variety of fruits is one important way to make sure they get all the goodness they need for tip-top growing. Seeing grown-ups eat fruit, too, means setting the best example. Here are four simple ways to make delicious fruit treats for everyone to enjoy at family mealtimes.

Mango + passion fruit trifles

serves 4 | prep 10 minutes | freeze me

4 slices of **brioche**, torn into pieces

1 **mango**, halved, stoned and flesh scooped out

Juice of 3 **clementines** and finely grated rind of ½ clementine

150 ml/5 fl oz **thick natural yogurt**

175 ml/6 fl oz **homemade custard** (see page 137), or **ready-made fresh custard**

2 **passion fruits**, halved

Arrange the brioche in 4 tumblers or sundae glasses. Blend the mango with the clementine juice, then stir in the rind. Spoon the mixture on top of the brioche.

Mix together the yogurt and custard and spoon on top of the mango mixture, then chill until ready to serve.

When ready, scoop out the seeds and flesh from the passion fruit and pile them on top of the trifles.

Poached vanilla + black pepper strawberries

serves 4 | prep 5 minutes | cook 10 minutes

400 ml/14 fl oz fresh **orange juice**

2 teaspoons **clear honey** or **maple syrup**

1 teaspoon **vanilla extract**

300 g/10½ oz **strawberries**, hulled, halved if large

Freshly ground **black pepper**

Cream, **yogurt** or **ice cream**, to serve

Put the orange juice, honey or maple syrup and vanilla in a pan over a medium heat and bring almost to the boil. Reduce the heat to low and simmer for 5–7 minutes until syrupy.

Add the strawberries and a grinding of black pepper and turn until the strawberries are coated in the syrup, then spoon them into a bowl and leave to cool. The poached strawberries will keep in the fridge, covered, for up to 3 days.

Spiced cherry, berry + apple stew

serves 4 | prep 5 minutes | cook 10 minutes | freeze me | 10+

350 g/12 oz **frozen stoned cherries**

100 g/3½ oz **frozen blueberries**

1 **apple**, peeled, cored and diced

3 tablespoons **apple juice**

5 **cloves**

½ **cinnamon stick**

Natural yogurt, to serve

Put all the ingredients except the yogurt in a small saucepan over a medium–high heat and bring almost to the boil, then reduce the heat to low and simmer for 10 minutes until the fruit has softened.

Leave the fruit to cool slightly, then remove the cloves and cinnamon stick. Serve warm or cold with natural yogurt.

Dippy fruit fondue

serves 4 | prep 10 minutes | freeze me

½ large **cantaloupe melon**, cut in half around its middle

About 200 g/7 oz **favourite fruit**, such as strawberries, peaches, grapes, raspberries, kiwi fruit, blueberries or nectarines

5 tablespoons fresh **orange juice**

For the fruity dipping sauce

250 g/9 oz **raspberries**

A good squeeze of **lime**

A drizzle of **clear honey** or **maple syrup**, to taste

Using a spoon, scoop the seeds out of the centre of the melon half. Slice a sliver off the base of the melon so that it stands up and place the melon on a serving plate. Scoop out most of the flesh with a melon baller to make a bowl shape with a 1-cm/½-in border.

Prepare your fruit (peeling, chopping, slicing and deseeding as necessary). Mix the fruit, including the melon balls, with the orange juice, then spoon it into the melon bowl, pouring over any juice.

To make the fruity dipping sauce, blend the raspberries with the lime juice. Taste and sweeten with honey or maple syrup as needed. To serve, either use cocktail sticks, little forks, or fingers to dunk the fruit from the melon bowl into the dipping sauce.

twinkle twinkle little star...

Starry night plum custards

Put some sparkle on the family table with these one-pot custards flavoured with warming cinnamon and bittersweet star anise. Eat them up and see how you glow!

What you need

Unsalted butter, for greasing

5 **plums**, halved, stoned and chopped

Finely grated rind and juice of 1 **orange**

For the vanilla custard

350 ml/12 oz **whole milk**

1 **cinnamon** stick

1 **star anise**

2 **eggs**, lightly beaten

1 teaspoon **vanilla extract**

2 tablespoons **clear honey**

Freshly grated **nutmeg**

What to do

1. Lightly grease 4–6 ramekins with butter. To make the custard, put the milk, cinnamon stick and star anise in a small saucepan over a medium–high heat and bring almost to the boil, stirring occasionally. Remove from the heat and leave for 10 minutes to infuse the milk with the spices.

2. Meanwhile, put the plums in a saucepan with the orange rind and juice and simmer for 10 minutes until cooked. Roughly mash with the back of a fork and set aside.

3. Preheat the oven to 170°C/325°F/Gas Mark 3. Using a hand whisk, whisk together the eggs, vanilla and honey until pale and creamy.

4. When the milk has had time to infuse, warm it briefly. Strain the milk, discarding the cinnamon and star anise, then gradually whisk it into the egg mixture.

5. Divide the plums among the prepared ramekins, then pour in the custard until almost to the top. Place in a baking tin and pour in enough just-boiled water to come two-thirds of the way up the sides of the ramekins. Grate a little nutmeg over each one, then carefully put the tin in the oven and bake for 25–30 minutes, or until the custards have set but are still slightly wobbly. Serve warm or cold.

Mmmm... macaroons

makes 12 • prep 10 minutes • cook 15 minutes • freeze me

Macaroons are a great way to use up any leftover egg whites. This easy recipe uses ground almonds instead of flour, which makes the macaroons gluten-free.

What you need

85 g/3 oz **unsweetened desiccated coconut**

30 g/1 oz **ground almonds**

30 g/1 oz **caster sugar**

2 large **egg whites**

12 dried **blueberries** or **sour cherries**

What to do

1. Preheat the oven to 200°C/400°F/Gas Mark 6. Line a baking sheet with baking parchment. Mix together the coconut, ground almonds and sugar.

2. Lightly whisk the egg whites in a large bowl until frothy, then stir in the coconut mixture.

3. Place 12 heaped tablespoons of the coconut mixture on the prepared baking sheet and top each with a blueberry or sour cherry. Bake for 10–12 minutes until light golden. Leave to cool slightly and firm up on the baking sheet before transferring to a wire rack to cool. Store in an airtight container for up to 3 days.

Coconut colours

Just for fun

Gather together some different food colourings. Put some desiccated coconut into little zip-lock bags, then add a different food colouring to each bag. Seal up the bags and give them all a good shake – multicoloured coconut! You can use the coconut for decorating cakes. Or (for more fun) give your little one a glue stick to 'draw' a pattern on a piece of paper, then dust over some coconut, and see the patterns appear as if by magic!

Fruit + veg animal fun

Making food look yummy on the plate is all part of the Ella's Kitchen mission to make food fun. The following ideas are easy for little ones to do for themselves – and there are no nasty pointy cocktail sticks that could hurt fingers! Of course, grown-ups will need to do the cutting and slicing.

Tasty green turtles

What you need

1 **kiwi fruit**, skinned and halved

4 **green grapes**

4 **tiny seeds** (such as nigella seeds)

What to do

☺ Slice the rounded ends off the two halves of kiwi fruit, just so that each half stands up on a plate, halved side upwards.

☺ Position a whole grape at one end of one kiwi half to make the turtle's head. Repeat with another grape for the other kiwi half. (Note that whole grapes can pose a choking hazard for very little ones.) Finally, cut the remaining grapes lengthways into quarters and position the quarters to create four little legs around each kiwi half.

☺ Finally, push two seeds into each grape 'head' to give the turtles eyes.

Fluttery berry butterfly

What you need

2 hulled **strawberries** (green tops reserved)

1 **blackberry**

What to do

☺ Position the blackberry on the plate to form the butterfly's body. Slice one strawberry around its circumference to create six round slices.

☺ Take the two biggest rounds of strawberry and position them either side of the bottom of the blackberry to form the bottoms of the butterfly's wings. Take two smaller rounds and pop them on top of the larger ones as 'spots'.

☺ Halve the remaining strawberry along its length and position the halves, cut-side up, pointed end inwards, either side of the blackberry to form the upper parts of the wings. Place the remaining small slices of strawberry on top of these to give the upper wings spots, too.

☺ Pull two little leaves from the reserved green tops and position them at the top of the blackberry for antennae.

Cauliflower + olive sheep

What you need

7 small **cauliflower** florets (cooked and cool enough to handle)

1 **black olive**

2 **sesame seeds**

What to do

☺ Put one cauliflower floret on a plate and arrange the remaining florets all the way around it to create the sheep's woolly coat.

☺ Halve the olive lengthways and put one half on top of the middle floret. This is the sheep's head.

☺ Cut two slices from the remaining olive half. Cut one slice in two to give you two 'arches'. Position these at the top of the head as two ears. Halve another olive slice and use these to make legs coming from the floret positioned beneath the sheep's head.

☺ Finally, position your sesame seeds on the sheep's head as two eyes (you can use teeny weeny pieces of cauliflower if you don't have any sesame seeds). Baaa!

Cherry, berry + apple bread pudding

serves 6–8 | prep 20 minutes | cook 40 minutes | freeze me | 10+
+ standing

This fruity bread pudding is beautifully light and airy – one scoop will never be enough! Made with wholemeal bread, it's better for you, too.

What you need

30 g/1 oz **unsalted butter**, plus extra for greasing

375 g/13 oz **wholemeal loaf**, cut into thickish slices, or **ready-sliced wholemeal bread**, crusts removed, each slice cut into 2 triangles

½ quantity **Spiced Cherry, Berry + Apple Stew** (see page 135)

3 **eggs**, lightly beaten

3 tablespoons **maple syrup**

1 teaspoon **vanilla extract**

600 ml/1 pint **whole milk**, warmed

1 teaspoon **demerara sugar** (optional)

Ground cinnamon, for dusting

What to do

1. Preheat the oven to 180°C/350°F/Gas Mark 4. Lightly grease a large, shallow ovenproof dish with butter. Butter the bread slices and arrange them in the dish, spooning the fruit sauce in between each slice of bread.

2. To make a custard, whisk together the eggs, maple syrup and vanilla, then gradually whisk in the warm milk. Pour the custard over the bread in the dish, pressing the bread down slightly. Leave to stand for 10 minutes, then scatter the demerara sugar over the top, if using.

3. Put the dish in a large baking tin, pour in enough hot water to come halfway up the sides of the tin, then carefully place it in the oven and bake for 25–30 minutes until the top is golden and the custard has just set. Dust with cinnamon before serving warm.

Squish, spoon + sprinkle

Can I help?

Arranging the bread, spooning over the fruit sauce and sprinkling the sugar are all easy-peasy jobs for any willing family sous-chefs.

Cinnamon + date rolys

Rolling up the pastry for these roly-polys is a good job for a little chef. We've used dates to make our swirls, but unsulphured dried apricots would be just as good.

What you need

150 g/5½ oz ready-to-eat **dried dates**

30 g/1 oz **unsalted butter**, softened

½ teaspoon **ground cinnamon**, plus extra for sprinkling

1 teaspoon **vanilla extract**

30 g/1 oz **flaked almonds**

320 g/11½ oz **ready-rolled puff pastry** sheet

1 **egg**, lightly beaten

What to do

1. Preheat the oven to 200°C/400°F/Gas Mark 6. Line 2 large baking sheets with baking parchment. Put the dates in a bowl and pour over enough just-boiled water to cover. Soak for 20 minutes until softened, then drain and blend together with the butter, cinnamon and vanilla to make a thick, smooth paste.

2. Unroll the pastry and spread the date paste over in an even layer, leaving a narrow border around the edge. Sprinkle over three-quarters of the almonds, then roll up the pastry tightly, starting from the long side.

3. Slice the pastry roll into 2-cm/¾-in thick rounds to make about 14 in total and place the rounds flat on the baking sheets. Using a rolling pin or your hand, flatten each round to about 1 cm/½ in thick. Brush the tops with beaten egg and scatter the remaining flaked almonds over. Bake for 25–30 minutes, or until risen and cooked through. Transfer to a wire rack to cool slightly, then enjoy either warm or cold. Store in an airtight container for up to 3 days.

Summer cooler popsicles

These lickable, frozen treats are just the thing to help the whole family cool down in the heat of summer (or anytime you fancy something chilly). You can substitute the fruit in the popsicles for any of your favourites.

What you need

1 large **mango**, peeled, stoned and cut into chunks (about 250 g/9 oz)

Juice of 1 **orange**, strained

1 tablespoon **maple syrup**

200 g/7 oz **strawberries**, hulled

150 ml/5 fl oz **coconut milk**

2 teaspoons **vanilla extract**

8 **lolly moulds**

What to do

(1) Blend together the mango, orange juice and maple syrup until puréed. Pour into a jug. Blend the strawberries separately until puréed. Combine the coconut milk and vanilla in a separate jug.

(2) Pour a little of the mango purée into the lolly moulds, followed by a little coconut milk mixture and then equal amounts of the strawberry purée. Top up with the rest of the coconut milk and mango purée to give a swirly pattern.

(3) Place the popsicles in the freezer and freeze for a couple of hours or so until solid.

Try this, too!

Our Spiced Cherry, Berry + Apple Stew recipe (see page 135) tastes great cooled completely, then swirled into thick natural yogurt and frozen.

For babies

From 10 months

Mash up half a popsicle (you may need to let it thaw for a bit first) in a bowl and feed it with a spoon.

Fruity iceberg bites

serves 8–10

prep 10 minutes

cook 5 minutes

freeze me

+ freezing

A superb alternative to ice cream, these little pieces of frozen yogurt are naturally flavoured with berries and have granola for a special crunch.

What you need

25 g/1 oz **unsweetened desiccated coconut**

350 ml/12 fl oz full-fat **Greek yogurt**

2 teaspoons **vanilla extract**

1 tablespoon **maple syrup** or **clear honey**

55 g/2 oz **Crunchy Coconut + Cranberry Granola** (see page 14) or ready-made **low-sugar granola**

100 g/3½ oz **frozen blueberries**, part-defrosted

100 g/3½ oz **strawberries**, or **favourite fresh or dried fruit**

What to do

1. Put the coconut in a large, dry frying pan and toast over a medium–low heat, tossing the pan, until light golden (about 3 minutes). Tip into a bowl and leave to cool.

2. Pour the yogurt into a separate large bowl and stir in the vanilla and maple syrup or honey, along with the granola, blueberries and toasted coconut and fold gently until it's all combined.

3. Line a small baking sheet with clingfilm, leaving enough overhanging to cover the tray. Tip the yogurt mixture into the tray and spread it out until it is about 1 cm/ ½ in thick. Scatter the strawberries over the top, pressing them down slightly. Fold the clingfilm over to cover and place in the freezer until solid.

4. To serve, remove from the freezer, leave the yogurt to soften slightly and then break into pieces. You can put any uneaten pieces in a freezer-proof tub and put them back in the freezer for up to 1 month.

149

Time for a family get-together!

Where's mine?

Whether you're cooking Sunday lunch for granny and grandpa or a special birthday celebration with all your family and friends, you'll find this chapter packed with tummy-filling crowd-pleasers.

Lazy-day lamb with tahini yogurt

serves 6–8 | prep 20 minutes | cook 4 hours | freeze me 10+

+ marinating

This tasty family feast is slow cooked, so it leaves you lots of time to join in with the party. It's a sociable dish – everyone piles in and wraps up their favourite food!

What you need

1.3 kg/3 lb **lamb shoulder** on the bone

2 **carrots**, peeled and quartered lengthways

1 **onion**, cut into wedges

1 long **rosemary** sprig

Pomegranate seeds, **mint** leaves, **flatbreads**, **lemon** wedges, and shredded **carrot** and **salad leaves**, to serve

For the marinade

1 tablespoon **mixed spice**

4 teaspoons **ground cumin**

3 **garlic** cloves, crushed

1 tablespoon **olive oil**

Finely grated rind and juice of 1 **lemon**

1 tablespoon **clear honey**

Freshly ground **black pepper**

For the tahini yogurt sauce (optional)

150 ml/5 fl oz **Greek yogurt**

2 tablespoons **tahini**

1 **garlic** clove, crushed

2 tablespoons **lemon** juice

What to do

1. Pat the lamb dry and make several slashes across the top. Mix together all the marinade ingredients and rub the mixture all over the lamb, making sure it gets into the cuts. Put the carrots, onion and rosemary in a roasting tin, top with the lamb, cover and marinate at room temperature for 1 hour.

2. Preheat the oven to its highest setting.

3. Add a good splash of water to the lamb tin, cover with a double layer of foil and put it in the oven. Immediately turn the oven temperature down to 160°C/315°F/Gas Mark 2–3 and roast for 3 hours.

4. Remove the foil, baste the lamb with any juices in the base of the tin and roast, uncovered, for another 1 hour until the lamb is very tender. Remove from the oven, cover with foil and a clean tea towel and leave to rest for 15 minutes.

5. Meanwhile, mix together all the ingredients for the tahini yogurt sauce and warm the flatbreads in the oven. Serve the lamb pulled into chunks, or shredded with forks, rather than carved. Skim off and discard any fat in the base of the roasting tin, then spoon some of the pan juices over the shredded lamb.

6. Place the lamb on a wooden board, scatter over the pomegranate seeds and mint leaves and serve with flatbreads, lemon wedges, tahini yogurt sauce and salad on the side.

153

Extra-special rosemary roast pork + apple sauce

serves 6-8 | prep 20 minutes | cook 2 hours | freeze me (sauce only)

This roast pork has all the best bits of a well-loved roast meal, with an extra-special herby flavour and *deeelicious* apple sauce. No fighting over the yummy crackling! Who's going to get the crispiest roast potato?

What you need

1.5 kg/3 lb 5 oz **boneless pork loin**, skin slashed and tied with string

1 teaspoon **sunflower oil**

2 **carrots**, peeled and quartered lengthways

1 **onion**, cut into wedges

2 long **rosemary sprigs**

Coarse **sea salt** and freshly ground **black pepper**

Roast potatoes, **gravy** and **veg**, to serve

For the special apple sauce

2 **apples**, peeled, cored and cut into chunks

1 **garlic** clove, crushed

4 tablespoons **extra virgin olive oil**

1 teaspoon **white wine vinegar**

1 tablespoon **clear honey**

Ella's shortcut

The apple sauce really is very special but if you needed a quick alternative, you could try 1 x 70 g pouch of Ella's Kitchen apples apples apples.

What to do

1. Take the pork out of the fridge 30 minutes before roasting. Preheat the oven to 240°C/475°F/Gas Mark 8. Pat dry the pork skin and rub with a little oil, then season with salt and pepper (the salt helps give crisp crackling).

2. Scatter the carrots and onion in a roasting tin. Sit the rosemary and then the pork on top. Roast the pork in the oven for 20 minutes, then reduce the heat to 180°C/350°F/Gas Mark 4 and cook for a further 1 hour 30 minutes, or until cooked to your liking.

3. Meanwhile, make the special apple sauce. Put the apples in a small saucepan and just cover with water, then cook for 10 minutes, or until tender. Drain the apples and put them in a mini food processor with the garlic and blend to a purée (or mash by hand). Gradually whisk in the olive oil, a few drops at a time, until you have a smooth, creamy sauce, then stir in the vinegar and honey.

4. Transfer the pork to a warm dish. If the crackling needs crisping up further, remove it from the meat, then cover the pork with foil to keep it warm. Turn the oven or grill to high and give the crackling a quick blast of heat. If the crackling is already crisp, don't cover with foil otherwise it will turn soggy. To serve the pork, remove the string and crackling, if you haven't already done so, and carve into slices. Serve with roast potatoes, gravy and vegetables.

Crispy topped pork stroganoff

serves 6–8 · prep 15 minutes · cook 50 minutes · 10+

A melt-in-your-mouth kind of dinner, this stroganoff is so good you'll be creating family gatherings just so you have a reason to make this big, wholesome dish. The rösti topping makes a brilliant alternative to mash, and gives the stroganoff a good crunch.

What you need

2 tablespoons **olive oil**

1 **onion**, chopped

2 **leeks**, chopped

250 g/9 oz **button mushrooms**, halved if large

500 g/1 lb 2 oz **pork shoulder or leg**, diced

1 heaped tablespoon **plain flour**

2 large **garlic** cloves, chopped

1 tablespoon chopped **rosemary**

2 **bay leaves**

2 teaspoons **mild smoked paprika**

300 ml/½ pint reduced-salt **chicken stock**

3 tablespoons **soured cream**

450 g/1 lb **new potatoes**, such as Charlotte

40 g/1½ oz **unsalted butter**, diced

Speed it up!

Use pork fillet instead of shoulder or leg and serve just the stroganoff mixture with rice or mash on the side, instead of baking with the rosti. All the deliciousness in less time!

What to do

1. Heat half the oil in a large saucepan over a medium heat. Add the onion, leeks and mushrooms and cook for 5 minutes, stirring, until softened. Remove from the pan with a slotted spoon and set aside.

2. Dust the pork in the flour. Pour the rest of the oil into the pan over a medium–high heat, add the pork and cook for 5 minutes, stirring, until browned all over. Return the vegetables to the pan with the garlic, herbs and paprika, then pour in the stock and stir until combined. Bring to the boil, then reduce the heat, part-cover with a lid and simmer for 15 minutes until the sauce has reduced and thickened. Remove the bay leaves, stir in the soured cream and warm through.

3. Meanwhile, preheat the oven to 200°C/400°F/Gas Mark 6. Cook the potatoes in a large saucepan of boiling water for 10–15 minutes until tender. Drain, then when cool enough to handle, peel off the skins and coarsely grate into a bowl. Gently stir in half the butter.

4. Spoon the pork mixture into a shallow, ovenproof dish, then spoon the potato mixture on top in an even layer. Dot the top with the remaining butter and cook in the oven for 25 minutes or until the top starts to turn golden.

Butterflied Indian chicken

serves 6–8 · prep 20 minutes · cook 40 minutes · freeze me

+ marinating

Spatchcocking a chicken (splitting it down the middle and opening it out) gives it a shape like a butterfly. Best of all, it takes less than half the roasting time of regular roast chicken.

What you need

1.8 kg/4 lb whole **chicken**

Chopped **red chillies**, for sprinkling (optional)

Apple Raita (see page 177), **carrot** and **red onion** salad, and warmed **naan**, to serve

For the marinade

3 **garlic** cloves, grated

2.5-cm/1-in piece of fresh **root ginger**, grated (no need to peel)

Finely grated rind of 1 **lemon**

2 teaspoons **garam masala**

1 teaspoon **paprika**

3 **cardamom pods**, seeds ground (optional)

1 teaspoon **ground cumin**

125 ml/4 fl oz **natural yogurt**

Freshly ground **black pepper**

When there's time

You don't have to spatchcock. You could coat the whole chicken in the marinade and marinate as in step 3, then roast at 180°C/350°F/Gas Mark 4 for 1½ hours, until the juices run clear.

What to do

1. Mix together all the ingredients for the marinade in a large, non-metallic bowl.

2. To spatchcock the chicken, put it breast-side down on a chopping board with the legs towards you. Locate the backbone, then using kitchen scissors or a sharp knife carefully cut down either side of the backbone to remove it. Open the chicken out like a butterfly and turn it over. With the heel of your palm, flatten the breastbone so the chicken is roughly the same thickness all over.

3. Put the chicken in the marinade bowl and turn to coat well in the marinade. Cover and leave in the fridge to marinate for at least 1 hour, preferably overnight.

4. Preheat a barbecue or grill to high. Insert 2 skewers diagonally crossways through the chicken to keep the bird flat. Put the chicken, breast-side down, on a barbecue or grill and cook for 20 minutes until the skin on top starts to turn crisp and golden. Brush the top with more of the marinade, then turn the chicken over and cook for another 20 minutes, or until cooked through and the juices run clear. Alternatively, cook the spatchcocked chicken in an oven preheated to 180°C/350°F/Gas Mark 4 for the same length of time.

5. Sprinkle the red chilli over the chicken for the adults, if you like. Serve with Apple Raita, carrot salad and naan breads on the side.

Four ways with veggies

It goes without saying that veggies are so important for keeping your whole family in tip-top health, but we know that steaming and boiling can get boring. Here are some ideas to put souped-up turbo veg on your family table.

serves 4 | prep 5 minutes | cook 10 minutes | freeze me | 10+

Creamy leeks

3 **leeks**, thinly sliced

½ teaspoon reduced-salt **vegetable bouillon powder** or ¼ **vegetable stock cube**

2 tablespoons **crème fraîche**

Put the leeks in a saucepan and just cover with water. Bring to the boil, then reduce the heat to low and simmer for 5–7 minutes until tender. Drain, reserving 3 tablespoons of the cooking water.

Put the leeks, reserved water, bouillon powder and crème fraîche into a blender and blend until smooth. Spoon the leeks back into the pan and reheat when needed.

serves 4 | prep 5 minutes | cook 15 minutes

Chinese 'seaweed'

4 large handfuls of **curly kale**, tough stalks removed and large pieces torn into bite-sized chunks

2 teaspoons **sesame oil**

1 teaspoon **black or toasted white sesame seeds**, to serve

Preheat the oven to 150°C/300°F/Gas Mark 2. Put the kale in a bowl, pour over the sesame oil and rub it into the kale with your fingers until coated. Tip the kale onto a large baking sheet and put in the oven for 15 minutes, turning halfway, until crisp. Keep an eye on it as it can easily burn.

Serve the 'seaweed' sprinkled with the sesame seeds.

Pink 'slaw

100 g/3½ oz **red cabbage**, shredded

1 **carrot**, peeled and coarsely grated

1 raw **beetroot**, peeled and coarsely grated

4 **sprouts**, outer leaves removed and coarsely grated

1 **eating apple** (skin on), cored and coarsely grated

For the yogurt dressing

100 ml/3½ fl oz **natural yogurt**

1 teaspoon **wholegrain mustard**

Juice of 1 small **lemon**

Mix together all the ingredients for the dressing.

Put the cabbage, carrot, beetroot, sprouts and apple in a serving bowl. Pour the dressing over the top and turn until combined. Serve straightaway.

Crispy courgette chips

20 g/¾ oz **ground almonds**

30 g/1 oz **Parmesan cheese**, finely grated

1 **egg**

2 **courgettes**, halved lengthways, then cut into long chips

Preheat the oven to 200°C/400°F/Gas Mark 6. Line a large baking sheet with baking parchment.

Mix together the ground almonds and Parmesan in a shallow bowl. Lightly beat the egg in a separate shallow bowl.

Dunk the courgette 'chips' into the egg followed by the ground almond mixture until coated. Place on the prepared baking sheet and roast for 30 minutes, turning once, or until golden and crisp.

Dig-in salmon lasagne

serves 6–8 | prep 20 minutes | cook 1 hour | freeze me | 10+

Salmon, broccoli, melty cheese and pasta… Yum! Open wide for every mouthful!

What you need

250 g/9 oz large **broccoli** florets

30 g/1 oz **unsalted butter**,
plus extra for greasing

2 **leeks**, finely chopped

2 **garlic** cloves, crushed

9 sheets of **dried egg lasagne**

500 g/1 lb 2 oz skinless, boneless
salmon fillets, thinly sliced

140 g/5 oz **Gruyère cheese**, grated

Green salad, to serve

For the béchamel sauce

70 g/2½ oz **unsalted butter**

70 g/2½ oz **plain flour**

750 ml/1¼ pints **whole milk**,
warmed

125 ml/4 fl oz reduced-salt **fish
stock**, warmed

Finely grated rind and juice of
1 **lemon**

1 teaspoon **Dijon mustard**

Freshly ground **black pepper**

What to do

1. To make the béchamel sauce, melt 70 g/
2½ oz of butter in a saucepan over a low
heat, stir in the flour and cook for 2 minutes,
stirring. Mix together the milk and stock
and gradually stir into the pan. Simmer for
5 minutes, or until the sauce thickens to the
consistency of double cream. Season with
pepper and stir in the lemon rind and juice
and the Dijon mustard. Set aside.

2. Meanwhile, steam the broccoli for 5 minutes
or until tender, then refresh under cold
running water, drain well and finely chop.

3. Melt the remaining butter in a large frying
pan over a medium–low heat. Add the leeks
and fry for 3 minutes until tender, then stir in
the garlic and chopped broccoli.

4. Preheat the oven to 180°C/350°F/Gas
Mark 4. To assemble the lasagne, butter a
large ovenproof dish, then spoon a quarter
of the béchamel into the base and cover with
3 sheets of lasagne, half the leek mixture and
half the salmon. Spoon another quarter of
the sauce into the dish and top with half the
cheese, 3 sheets of lasagne, the remaining
leek mixture and the rest of the salmon.
Spoon in another quarter of the sauce, cover
with the last 3 sheets of lasagne, the remaining
sauce and a final topping of cheese.

5. Bake the lasagne for 40–45 minutes until the
top is golden and the pasta is cooked. Serve
with a green salad.

163

Party popper veggie pie

serves 8–10 · prep 20 minutes · cook 1¼ hours · freeze me

Packed with colour, like the streamers in a party popper, this veggie pie requires a bit of time and love, but the results will bring squeals of delight – perfect for a family celebration!

What you need

2 tablespoons **olive oil**, plus extra for brushing

1 large **butternut squash**, peeled, deseeded and cut into chunks (600 g/1 lb 5 oz prepared weight)

300 g/10½ oz **cranberry sauce**

Finely grated rind of 1 small **orange**

30 g/1 oz **unsalted butter**

2 **leeks**, trimmed and finely chopped

250 g/9 oz **chestnut mushrooms**, finely chopped

3 **garlic** cloves, chopped

175 g/6 oz **cooked chestnuts**, finely chopped

1 teaspoon **Dijon mustard**

2 teaspoons **thyme** leaves

1 tablespoon chopped **rosemary**

1 teaspoon **vegetable bouillon powder**

200 g/7 oz **cooked puy or green lentils** (if using canned lentils, make sure you drain them well first)

270-g/9¾-oz pack of **filo pastry**, 46 × 23 × 6-cm/18 × 9 × 2½-in sheets

Freshly ground **black pepper**

What to do

1. Preheat the oven to 200°C/400°F/Gas Mark 6. Lightly grease a 23-cm/9-in springform cake tin with oil.

2. Toss the squash in half the oil, then spread it out in an even layer in a roasting tin. Roast the squash, turning halfway, for 20 minutes or until tender. Remove from the oven and blend to a purée, then set aside.

3. While the squash is cooking, mix together the cranberry sauce and orange rind and set aside.

4. Meanwhile, heat the butter and remaining oil in a large frying pan. Add the leeks and mushrooms and cook for 10 minutes until tender and there is no trace of liquid. Add the garlic, chestnuts, mustard, herbs, bouillon powder and cooked lentils. Season with pepper and cook for 3 minutes until heated through, then roughly mash the mixture in the pan with a potato masher until you have a coarse paste. Leave to cool slightly.

5. To assemble, place the prepared cake tin on a baking sheet. Take a sheet of filo and place it in half of the cake tin with any surplus hanging over the edges. Brush it with olive oil and place the second sheet of filo, slightly overlapping, in the other half of the tin and brush it with oil. Turn the tin and repeat with another 2 layers, again brushing them with oil. Turn the tin and repeat with the final 2 layers, brushing with oil, so the excess pastry hangs evenly over the edge of the tin.

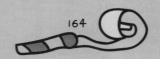

6 Spoon half of the mushroom mixture into the tin, pressing it down in an even layer, top with the squash, the remaining mushroom mixture and finally the cranberry sauce, making sure each layer is evenly spread out. Fold the excess layers of pastry over the top to cover the cranberry, scrunching it as you go – it shouldn't look too neat. Brush the top with oil and oven bake for 25 minutes.

7 Take the pie out of the oven, carefully remove the side of the cake tin, brush the side of the pie with oil and return it to the oven for another 20–25 minutes until golden all over. Leave the pie to sit for 10 minutes before cutting it into slices – you can serve it warm or at room temperature.

Open a restaurant
(at home)

Eating in a restaurant is always a treat – and now you can create a restaurant at home. Giving mealtimes a sense of occasion is a brilliant way to engage children with the fun of eating together, and they'll love the role play, too!

1

Decide on the basics

Think of a name for your restaurant and decide what's on the menu. Together, pick your favourite recipes from this book (limit options if you need to) and then give every chosen dish a name that's personal, like 'Mummy's Mega Meatballs' or 'Max's Razzle Dazzle Stew'.

2

Get creative

Grab some card and all your colouring and sticking gear. Your restaurant will need a sign, and a really delicious-looking menu card. Cut and stick from magazines and newspapers. Make your menu look *reeeally* appetising!

Lay the table

Lay out the cutlery and crockery, and then add some personal touches. Could you theme your restaurant? Italian, Caribbean, Chinese; shabby chic or farmyard style? Gather props to bring your theme to life. Personalized name cards and hand-decorated paper napkins or tablecloths (see page 60) will add to the unique feel.

Set the mood

Create a restaurant ambience – pick some flowers from the garden and put them in a little vase on the table. Discuss your ambient music options and – for added fun – let your children choose the playlist.

Use role play

It's almost time to open. Give everyone a role. Who will greet diners; who is the chef, or the waiter? Once the food is served, everyone is a guest. Who do you imagine sitting at the next table? What do you think of the service and the food? Don't forget to pay the bill before you leave! When you're done, it's everyone's job to help clear up!

167

Slowly-does-it beef pot roast

serves 6–8 | prep 15 minutes | cook 3 hours | freeze me | 10+

If you've got people coming over, you can get this slow-roast, melt-in-the-mouth beef in the oven and still have plenty of time to entertain friends and family and play with the kids. We love that kind of food!

What you need

2 tablespoons **olive oil**

1 kg/2 lb 4 oz **silverside or topside beef joint**

3 **carrots**, peeled, halved and quartered lengthways

1 large **onion**, halved and cut into wedges

1 **celery** stick, thickly sliced

2 **turnips**, halved and cut into wedges

3 **bay leaves**

4 **thyme** sprigs

3 **garlic** cloves, crushed

200 ml/7 fl oz **cranberry juice**

350 ml/12 fl oz reduced-salt **beef stock**

2 teaspoons **plain flour**

15 g/½ oz **unsalted butter**

Mashed or baked **potatoes**, to serve

What to do

1. Preheat the oven to 160°C/315°F/Gas Mark 3. Heat half the oil in a large, flameproof casserole over a medium–high heat and brown the beef for 8 minutes, turning it occasionally, until browned all over.

2. Remove the beef from the casserole, add the remaining oil and sauté the carrots, onion, celery and turnips for 5 minutes until softened. Add the bay leaves, thyme, garlic, cranberry juice and stock and stir to loosen any bits that have stuck to the base of the casserole. Bring to the boil, return the beef to the casserole, spoon over the gravy, cover with the lid and place in the oven for 2 hours 30 minutes, turning the beef halfway.

3. Remove the casserole from the oven. Take out the beef and vegetables and place on a warmed plate and cover with foil. To thicken the gravy, place the casserole on the hob over a medium heat, whisk in the flour and cook for 10 minutes until reduced and thickened, then stir in the butter until melted. Snip off the string around the beef and cut into slices, then serve with the vegetables, gravy and mashed or baked potatoes.

Time for the great outdoors!

Food outdoors is such fun, especially when there are lots of you to eat and play. We can't promise sunshine, but we can promise some yummy ideas for picnics and barbecues with family and friends!

Laid-back crustless quiche

serves 8–12 | prep 10 minutes | cook 40 minutes | freeze me | 10+

With potatoes on the inside, this quiche is filling even without a pastry casing! Take it on a family picnic, or put it in packed lunch for nursery, school or work.

What you need

350 g/12 oz **new potatoes**, halved if large

Unsalted butter, for greasing

8 **eggs**, lightly beaten

7 **spring onions**, sliced

100 g/3½ oz **sun-dried tomatoes** in oil, drained and chopped

A handful of **basil** leaves

1 tablespoon **oregano** or **thyme** leaves

175 ml/6 fl oz **whole milk**

140 g/5 oz **Gruyère cheese**, grated

Freshly ground **black pepper**

What to do

1. Boil the potatoes for 10–15 minutes until tender. Drain and cool slightly, then remove the skins and cut into bite-sized chunks.

2. Grease and line a 23-cm/9-in square cake tin. Preheat the oven to 180°C/350°F/Gas Mark 4.

3. Beat the eggs in a large bowl and add the rest of the ingredients, including the cooked potatoes. Season, and stir to combine. Pour the mixture into the prepared tin and bake for 35–40 minutes until set. Cool for 5 minutes, then turn out of the tin and cut into squares.

Find it!

Just for fun

A family picnic is the perfect opportunity for a scavenger hunt that tunes in to the sights, sounds and scents of the great outdoors. Make a list of items for everyone to find – try to think of one or two for each sense. Here are some ideas:

☺ Touch: a smooth stone + a rough leaf

☺ Smell: a flower + tree bark

☺ Sight: something yellow + something speckled

☺ Sound: a crunchy leaf + a snapping stick

☺ Taste: a blackberry (ensure an adult checks this before anything goes into little mouths)

Dino ribs in Chinese sauce

serves 6–8 · prep 10 minutes · cook 50 minutes · freeze me
+ chilling

We'd battle a hungry herd of dinosaurs for these ribs – they're that good! Cook them on the barbecue or in the oven until the meat falls off the bone and the marinade is sticky sweet. Irresistible!

What you need

1.5 kg/3 lb 5 oz individual meaty **pork ribs**

10 **peppercorns**

2 **bay leaves**

3 **star anise**

1 **onion**, sliced

3 **spring onions**, thinly sliced on diagonal

Rice and **steamed pak choi** or **salad**, to serve

For the marinade

150 ml/5 fl oz **hoisin sauce**

1 tablespoon **clear honey**

Juice of 1 **orange**

1 tablespoon **white wine vinegar**

2 teaspoons **Chinese 5-spice powder**

What to do

1. Put the ribs in a large pan and pour in enough cold water to cover, add the peppercorns, bay leaves, star anise and onion. Bring to the boil, cover with a lid and simmer for 30 minutes. Drain, discarding the flavourings, and put the ribs in a large non-metallic bowl.

2. Meanwhile, mix together all the ingredients for the marinade, pour it over the ribs and turn until they are coated all over. Leave to cool, then cover and chill in the fridge for at least 1 hour, overnight if time allows.

3. Preheat the barbecue or grill to high. Grill the ribs for 20 minutes, basting occasionally with the marinade. (Alternatively, preheat the oven to 200°C/400°F/Gas Mark 6. Line two baking sheets with foil, arrange the ribs on top, baste with the marinade, and roast for 35–40 minutes until golden and sticky. Turn the ribs halfway and baste with more of the marinade.)

4. Pile the ribs up in a bowl, sprinkle with spring onions and serve with pak choi and rice.

Learn to weigh

Can I help?

Little helpers will love measuring out the marinade ingredients and stirring them together. Let them help you stir the ribs through to fully coat them, too.

Nibbly apple + cranberry oat biscuits

makes 12 | prep 10 minutes | cook 35 minutes | freeze me

These oat biscuits are free from any refined sugar making them a good choice for an in-between snack. Pop them in a lunchbox or picnic hamper as a nibbly treat.

What you need

2 **eating apples**, peeled, cored and roughly chopped

70 g/2½ oz **porridge oats**

70 g/2½ oz **wholemeal plain flour**

½ teaspoon **bicarbonate of soda**

1 teaspoon **mixed spice**

70 g/2½ oz **dried cranberries**

70 g/2½ oz **unsalted butter**

2 tablespoons **clear honey**

Ella's shortcut

If you need to save time, use 1 x 70 g pouch of Ella's Kitchen apples apples apples in place of the cooked apples.

What to do

1. Preheat the oven to 180°C/350°F/Gas Mark 4. Line a large baking tray with baking parchment.

2. Put the apples in a pan over a medium heat and pour in just enough water to cover. Part-cover with a lid and cook the apples for 15 minutes, or until tender, then drain well. Put the apple in a bowl and mash with the back of a fork until smooth, then set aside.

3. Mix together the oats, flour, bicarbonate of soda, mixed spice and cranberries. Stir in 70 g/2½ oz of the apple purée.

4. Melt the butter in a small pan over a low heat, stir in the honey, then pour the mixture into the dry ingredients and mix together until combined.

5. Place 12 heaped tablespoons of the mixture on the prepared baking tray, spacing each spoonful evenly apart. Flatten the top of each spoonful slightly with the back of a fork. Bake the biscuits for 17–20 minutes, or until golden.

6. Leave to cool on the baking tray for a couple of minutes, then transfer the biscuits to a wire rack to cool completely. Eat them just as they are, or serve topped with a little of the remaining apple sauce.

Five ways to dip + dunk

Kids love dipping and dunking. These dips make excellent picnic or lunchbox fillers. Serve them with breadsticks or veggie batons, or spread them on toast, which you then cut into crustless fingers for babies over 7 months.

Roasted carrot dip

serves 6–8 | prep 10 minutes | cook 50 minutes | freeze me | 7+

1 **sweet potato** (about 250 g/9 oz total weight)

3 large **carrots**, peeled and quartered lengthways

3 tablespoons **extra virgin olive oil**

1 **garlic** clove, crushed

2 tablespoons **tahini**

½–1 teaspoon **ras el hanout** or **harissa** (optional)

Juice of 1 **lemon**

Preheat the oven to 200°C/400°F/Gas Mark 6. Bake the sweet potato in the oven for 50 minutes, or until tender.

Meanwhile, toss the carrots in 1 tablespoon of the oil to coat, tip them onto a baking sheet in an even layer and roast (in the same oven as the potato) for 35–40 minutes, until tender and starting to colour. Peel the sweet potato and put the flesh in a food processor with the roasted carrots and the rest of the ingredients and blend until smooth and creamy.

Tunasalata

serves 6–8 | prep 10 minutes | cook 10 minutes | 10+

175 g/6 oz **potato**, peeled and cut into small chunks, or **stale crustless bread**

Juice of 1 **lemon** and finely grated rind of ½ lemon

½ small **onion**, finely grated

1 tablespoon **mayonnaise**

200 g/7 oz can **tuna chunks** in olive oil, drained, reserving the oil (supplement with **extra virgin olive oil**, if insufficient oil in the can)

Freshly ground **black pepper**

If using potato, cook the cubes in a pan of boiling water for 10 minutes or until tender, then drain and tip into a large bowl. Add 3 tablespoons of the oil from the fish and the lemon juice and mash until smooth. Add the onion, lemon rind, mayonnaise and tuna to the potato mixture and mash with a fork until combined, then season with pepper to taste.

If using bread, soak it briefly in cold water until soft, then drain and squeeze out any excess water. Place in a blender with the rest of the ingredients and blend until smooth, then season with pepper to taste.

Apple raita

serves 4 · prep 10 minutes · 10+

1 **red eating apple** (skin on), cored and coarsely grated

3 heaped tablespoons chopped **mint**

Juice of ½ **lime**

125 ml/4 fl oz **natural yogurt**

1 small **garlic** clove, crushed (optional)

Mix together all the ingredients for the raita in a bowl, adding the garlic, if using, and mixing again to combine.

Minty pea + ricotta dip

serves 6–8 · prep 10 minutes · cook 5 minutes · freeze me · 10+

175 g/6 oz **frozen peas**

100 g/3½ oz **ricotta cheese**

2 **spring onions**, thinly sliced

Juice and finely grated rind of 1 **lemon**

6 heaped tablespoons roughly chopped **mint**

4 tablespoons **natural yogurt**

Cook the peas in a pan of boiling water until tender (about 5 minutes), then drain and tip them into a blender with the ricotta, spring onions, lemon juice, mint and yogurt. Blend everything together until smooth and creamy. Spoon the dip into a bowl and stir in the lemon rind.

Smoky aubergine dip

serves 4 · prep 10 minutes · cook 45 minutes · freeze me · 7+

1 **aubergine**

1 tablespoon **olive oil**

1 small **garlic** clove, crushed

1 tablespoon **tahini**

3 tablespoons **natural yogurt**

½ teaspoon **mild smoked paprika**

Juice of ½ **lemon**

2 tablespoons finely chopped **flat-leaf parsley**

Preheat the oven to 200°C/400°F/Gas Mark 6. Prick the aubergine all over with a fork and then brush with a little of the oil. Place the aubergine on a baking sheet and roast for 45 minutes, or until the flesh is nice and soft. Cut the aubergine in half, scoop out the flesh, discarding any particularly seedy bits. Mash or blend the aubergine with the remaining oil, and the garlic, tahini, yogurt, paprika and lemon juice. Stir in the parsley and spoon into a bowl.

Sizzling steak niçoise salad

serves 6–8 · prep 15 minutes · cook 25 minutes

Seven different veggies mixed with eggs and meat make this salad a perfectly balanced meal for everyone. With so many tastes and textures, every mouthful is an adventure!

What you need

450 g/1 lb **new potatoes**, scrubbed and halved if large

140 g/5 oz fine **green beans**, cut into thirds

2 **corn-on-the-cobs**, husks removed, or 175 g/6 oz no-salt, no-sugar canned **sweetcorn**

85 g/3 oz **baby spinach leaves**, tough stalks removed

6 **tomatoes**, deseeded and diced

55 g/2 oz pitted **black olives**

½ **red onion**, thinly sliced

450 g/1 lb **steak**, at room temperature

4 hard-boiled **eggs**, peeled and each one quartered

For the dressing

6 tablespoons **extra virgin olive oil**, plus extra for cooking

Juice of 1 **lemon**

1 teaspoon **Dijon mustard**

20 g/¾ oz **Parmesan cheese**, finely grated, plus extra to serve

Freshly ground **black pepper**

What to do

1. Cook the potatoes in a pan of boiling water for 10–15 minutes until tender. Drain and set aside.

2. Meanwhile, steam the green beans for 5 minutes until tender, then refresh under cold running water. Steam the corn for 2 minutes, or until starting to soften, then drain and pat dry. Set aside the beans.

3. If using corn-on-the cob, brush the corn with oil and barbecue or griddle over a medium–high heat for 10 minutes, turning occasionally, until coloured in places. Stand the cob upright and slice the kernels off the cob and set aside. While the corn is cooking, mix together all the ingredients for the dressing and set aside.

4. To assemble the salad, arrange the spinach, cooked potatoes and green beans, and the tomatoes, olives and red onion on a serving platter. Scatter the corn kernels (or drained canned sweetcorn) over the top. Spoon some of the dressing over and toss until combined.

5. Brush the steak with oil and season. Barbecue or griddle over a medium–high heat, turning twice, for 5 minutes or until cooked to your liking. Leave to rest for 5 minutes, then cut into strips and arrange on top of the salad. Top with the quartered hard-boiled eggs and shave over some Parmesan, adding more dressing, if needed.

Stacked-up chicken + quinoa burgers

serves 8 | prep 15 minutes + chilling | cook 25 minutes | freeze me (cooked or uncooked)

Quinoa is a super-grain packed full of protein, fibre and iron – the basic stuff little ones need to grow and stay strong. Mixed with chicken and served in a bun with zingy pepper relish, it turns a humble chicken burger into a super-grain superstar!

What you need

- 50 g/1¾ oz **quinoa** (or 165 g/ 5¾ oz **ready-cooked quinoa**)
- 550 g/1 lb 4 oz skinless, boneless **chicken thighs**
- 1 **onion**, coarsely grated
- 2 teaspoons dried **thyme**
- 2 **garlic** cloves, finely chopped
- 100 g/3½ oz **roasted red pepper** from a jar, drained, patted dry and diced
- 3 tablespoons chopped **parsley**
- 1 **egg**, lightly beaten
- **Sunflower oil**, for cooking
- 8 **burger buns**, split in half and toasted
- Favourite **salad veg**, to serve

What to do

1. Put the quinoa in a saucepan, cover with water and bring to the boil. Reduce the heat, cover and simmer for 15–18 minutes until tender. Drain and leave to cool.

2. Meanwhile, finely chop the chicken in a food processor, spoon it into a bowl and combine with the onion, thyme, garlic, red pepper, parsley and cooled quinoa. Stir in the egg until everything is combined.

3. With wet hands, form the mixture into 8 burgers. Place the burgers on a plate, cover and chill in the fridge for 30 minutes. Brush the burgers with oil and barbecue for 3–4 minutes on each side. Alternatively, cook in a frying pan in the same way. Place the burgers in toasted buns with the Red Pepper Relish (see box, below), if you like, and serve with your favourite salad.

Red pepper relish

Mix together 150 g/5½ oz diced roasted red pepper, the juice of 1 lime, ½ diced red onion, 4 tablespoons of chopped parsley or basil and a splash of extra virgin olive oil. It's a relish to relish!

From 10 months

For babies

Little ones can enjoy a bun-less burger as long as it is chopped or mashed up well.

Crisp + crunchy cauliflower tabbouleh

serves 6–8 | prep 15 minutes | cook 20 minutes | freeze me
+ chilling

Tabbouleh is a traditional Middle Eastern salad made using bulgar wheat, but we've used quinoa for a yummy twist. It makes a filling meal in a bowl by itself, or a good side dish at a picnic or barbecue.

What you need

85 g/3 oz **quinoa** (or 225 g/8 oz **ready-cooked quinoa**)

5 large **cauliflower** florets, coarsely grated

9-cm/3½-in piece of **cucumber**, quartered lengthways, deseeded and diced

150 g/5½ oz **tomatoes**, deseeded and diced

3 handfuls of chopped **mint**

3 handfuls of chopped **parsley**

5 **spring onions**, finely chopped

2 **nectarines**, stoned and chopped

3 tablespoons toasted **pumpkin seeds**

For the dressing

3 tablespoons **extra virgin olive oil**

Finely grated rind of ½ large **lemon** and juice of 1 lemon

1 **garlic** clove, crushed

What to do

1. Put the quinoa in a saucepan, cover with water and bring to the boil over a high heat. Reduce the heat to medium–low, cover with a lid and simmer for 15–18 minutes until tender. Drain and put in a serving bowl.

2. Meanwhile, mix together the ingredients for the dressing.

3. Add the rest of the ingredients to the serving bowl with the quinoa, pour the dressing over and turn gently until combined. Finely chop the pumpkin seeds if serving to young children, then scatter over the salad. Serve at room temperature for the best flavour.

Sprinkled Brazilian pineapple sticks

Put on your carnival hat and have a festival with these griddled pineapple chunks. Who in the family can dance the best samba?

What you need

1 small **pineapple**

Clear honey, for brushing

A handful of **goji berries**, for sprinkling (optional)

Coconut yogurt or **thick natural yogurt**, to serve

For the coconut sprinkle

4 tablespoons **unsweetened desiccated coconut**

1 tablespoon **sesame seeds**

40 g/1½ oz **cashew nuts**

½ teaspoon **ground cinnamon**

What to do

1. Soak 4 wooden skewers in cold water for 30 minutes (or use metal skewers). Heat the barbecue or preheat the grill to high. Remove the leafy top of the pineapple and then stand the pineapple upright on a chopping board. Slice off the skin, then cut the pineapple into quarters lengthways. Remove the hard core, then cut each quarter into 1-cm/½-in thick slices.

2. Thread the pineapple onto the prepared skewers – about 8 pieces on each skewer. Barbecue or grill the pineapple for 5 minutes. Lightly brush with honey and cook for another 5 minutes, turning occasionally.

3. Meanwhile, make the coconut sprinkle. Toast the coconut in a dry frying pan for 2 minutes, or until it starts to colour, tossing occasionally. Tip into a bowl. Toast the sesame seeds in the same pan for 3 minutes, or until starting to colour. Add them to the coconut. Toast the cashews for 4 minutes, turning once, or until slightly golden. Finely chop the cashews and add to the bowl with the cinnamon, then stir to combine.

4. Sprinkle the pineapple with coconut sprinkle and with goji berries, if using, and serve with yogurt on the side. Alternatively, spoon some yogurt into a bowl, and top with pineapple chunks, goji berries, if using, and sprinkle.

Index

189

Thank you

A big thank you to all of the Ella's Kitchen employees and friends who contributed recipe ideas for this book and 'road-tested' them with their own families.

A huge thank you to Great Little Trading Company, MADE.COM, Anorak and Habitat for their kind supply of colourful props, which helped make our photos all the more lovely.

www.gltc.co.uk

www.made.com

www.anorakonline.co.uk

www.habitat.co.uk

A special thank you to all our little helpers – and their parents and carers – for their patience in front of the camera. Here's a list of our little stars and their ages on the days of our photoshoots.

Aaron Gormley (1 year) • Alfie Shaddick (1 year) • Amy Powell (2 years) • Anima Tavares (2 years) • Archie Beighton (2 years) • Arthur Jarrett (4 years) • Belle Birds (8 years) • Carter-Jai Moka (4 years) • Charlie Mortimore (1 year) • Creedan-Lee Moka (2 years) • Dexter Baker (1 year) • Eliza Worrall (1 year) • Ellie Heath (4 years) • Elliot Gunawardena (7 years) • Elliot Tilston (1 year) • Emily Morris (2 years) • Emily Shaddick (5 years) • Evangelina Maestri (1 year) • Flora Dugan (3 years) • Florence Lucas (3 years) • Frankie McGhee (2 years) • Freya Hambly (2 years) • Gavaani Sandu (1 year) • Gurshan Sandhu (7 years) • Hollie Brown (3 years) • Isla Venton (2 years) • Jalen Ogunbambi (4 years) • Jasmine Layla Bryan (2 years) • Jac Crosse (4 year) • Jacob Brown (4 years) • Jacob Parsons (2 years) • Jamie Livingston (6 years) • Juno Eccleston (4 years) • Katharine English (2 years) • Kyrell King-Allen (3 years) • Larina Larin-Alabi (4 years) • Layla Rooney (5 years) • Leelah Bousa (4 years) • Leo Dexter (3 years) • Leo Flouch (1 year) • Lottie Livingston (7 years) • Luca Nasser (3 years) • Lucy Heath (1 year) • Marlene Bousa (2 years) • Max Jun Li Lam (2 years) • Max Shaddick (1 year) • Maya Flouch (3 years) • Megan Crosse (5 years) •

Merryn Bray (2 years) • Nathan Brown (7 months) • Oli Mortimore (6 years) • Olivia Worrall (4 years) • Ollie Spurr (2 years) • Orla Sarsfield (4 years) • Owen Tilston (3 years) • Param Sandu (6 years) • Poppy Cameron (5 years) • Raffaele Maestri (4 years) • Rosie Venton (2 years) • Ruben Brown (2 years) • Ruby Rooney (4 years) • Sam English (4 years) • Sam Spurr (7 months) • Sebastian Bodey (2 years) • Sienna Parsons (2 years) • Summer Parsons (2 years) • Summer Turner (4 years) • Ted Gelling (1 year) • Theo Nasser (2 years) • Thomas Morris (6 months) • Tristan Bray (1 year) • Una Gormley (3 years) • Wilfred Jarrett (1 year) • Willis Birds (5 years) • Willow Bodey (6 months) • Zach Parsons (1 year)

And to the mums, dads, aunts, uncles and grandparents who let us take photos of them, too:

Amy Bodey • Amy Tilston • Andrea Baynton • Anita Sandu • Anna Shaddick • Daniel Flouch • Danielle Brown • David Tilston • Ellen Jarrett • Ellie Venton • Emily Maestri • Geoff Brown • Grahame Rooke • Harsha Gunawardena • Helen Brown • Jane Lloyd • Jez Birds • Jules Worrall • Julie Rooke • Junior Moka • Kate Birds • Katie Cameron • Kristina Nasser • Lai Chun Lee • Liz Sarsfield • Lorna Baker • Mark Heath • Nigel Lloyd • Peter Johnston • Rachel Heath • Rich Worrall • Roger Baynton • Rosie Parsons • Sadia Rooney • Sandra English • Sian Spurr • Sonali Flouch • Susie Feest • Timothy Feest • William Spurr

For letting us take photos at their homes, and for all the other important stuff we needed for our *Easy Family Cookbook*:

Judy Barratt
Claire Baseley
Justine Davies
Claire Dugan
Sarah Ford
Anita Mangan
Pippa Morton
Celia Pearman
Angie Turner
Ollie Woodall